Praise for *Country*...

'Brilliant.'
–*The Sydney Morning Herald*

'Bringing Gammage and Pascoe together is certainly a coup ... An urgent call to arms – an essential update of key findings from their earlier work, an instruction manual on the use of fire in caring for country, and a plea to trust Indigenous knowledge and local communities before large corporations or institutions.'
–Mark McKenna, *The Age*

'Reading the book excites me to want to act to care for land, and respectfully celebrate Indigenous knowledges. If you have a desire to be part of the action, then this book is for you.'
–Taylor Coyne, *The Conversation*.

'Authors Bill Gammage and Bruce Pascoe have joined forces to give substance to what many have begun to see, especially since the Black Summer of 2019–2020: the lessons of First Nations land management and fire control are essential to sustainability.'
–Judith White, *CultureHeist*

'A timely and important publication, given the recent debate about this country's history and the contribution to its understanding by this book's co-author, Bruce Pascoe.

'It offers two idiosyncratic voices – sometimes at odds, other times simpatico – and often talking past each other as to what urgently needs to change.

'Margo Neale's introduction highlights the complexities and opportunities of the current re-examination of Australia's past.

'Their message is clear: the time has come to reckon with our history...'
—Lynette Russell AM

Danielle Gorogo, *Flaming Trees*, 2020

Flaming Trees, the artwork detail used on the cover of this book and reproduced here in black and white, is one of four paintings that depicts the change in the environment and landscape since the arrival of Europeans in Australia.

Danielle Gorogo is a Clarence Valley First Nations artist living in the Northern Rivers region of New South Wales. She is a direct descendant of the Dunghutti, Gumbaynggirr and Bundjalung nations. Danielle's multifaceted cultural heritage, which includes First Nations Australian, Papua New Guinean, Māori and Micronesian ancestry, is reflected in her art.

COUNTRY

Aboriginal and Torres Strait Islander peoples are advised that this book contains the names of people who have passed away.

The stories in this book are shared with the permission of the original storytellers.

COUNTRY
Future Fire, Future Farming

BILL GAMMAGE
& BRUCE PASCOE

First published in Australia in 2021
by Thames & Hudson Australia Pty Ltd
11 Central Boulevard, Portside Business Park
Port Melbourne, Victoria 3207
ABN: 72 004 751 964

thamesandhudson.com.au

Country © Thames & Hudson Australia 2021

Introduction © Margo Neale/NMA 2021
Text © Bill Gammage and Bruce Pascoe 2021
Images © copyright remains with the individual copyright holders

24 23   5 4 3

The moral rights of the authors have been asserted.

All rights reserved. No part of this publication may be reproduced or transmitted in any form or by any means, electronic or mechanical, including photocopy, recording or any other information storage or retrieval system, without prior permission in writing from the publisher.

Any copy of this book issued by the publisher is sold subject to the condition that it shall not by way of trade or otherwise be lent, resold, hired out or otherwise circulated without the publisher's prior consent in any form or binding or cover other than that in which it is published and without a similar condition including these words being imposed on a subsequent purchaser.

Thames & Hudson Australia wishes to acknowledge that Aboriginal and Torres Strait Islander people are the first storytellers of this nation and the traditional custodians of the land on which we live and work. We acknowledge their continuing culture and pay respect to Elders past, present and future.

Thames & Hudson Australia thanks Professor Lynette Russell AM, ARC Kathleen Fitzpatrick Laureate Fellow, Monash Indigenous Studies Centre, for providing editorial advice.

The publisher gratefully acknowledges the Traditional Owners for McArthur River, Barrow Creek and Ngukurr (Roper River), Northern Territory; Central Land Council, Alice Springs; *Ngukurr News*, Ngukurr; Papulu Apparr-kari Aboriginal Corporation, Tennant Creek; and Museums Victoria, Melbourne, for assistance with community consultations and permissions to publish the images of artefacts and breads on pages 62–3.

978 1 76076 155 4 (paperback)
978 1 76076 215 5 (ebook)

 A catalogue record for this book is available from the National Library of Australia

Every effort has been made to trace accurate ownership of copyrighted text and visual materials used in this book. Errors or omissions will be corrected in subsequent editions, provided notification is sent to the publisher.

  This project has been assisted by the Australian Government through the Australia Council, its arts funding and advisory body.

First Knowledges is a series that complements the National Museum of Australia's Clever Country online videos.

Front cover: *Flaming Trees* by Danielle Gorogo

Series editor: Margo Neale
Cover design: Nada Backovic
Typesetting: Megan Ellis
Printed and bound in Australia by McPherson's Printing Group

 FSC® is dedicated to the promotion of responsible forest management worldwide. This book is made of material from FSC®-certified forests and other controlled sources.

To Australia

NOTE ON STYLE AND SPELLING

The First Knowledges series seeks to honour the individual voices and stylistic preferences of each book's authors. Readers may also note that for different language groups, variant spellings occur for similar words, cultural groups or names.

ON FIRE

The authors invite readers to reflect on the message from the contrasting photographs inside this book's covers. Pictured at the front is the cool burning of spinifex by Warlpiri people in the Northern Territory's Tanami Desert. At the back is an image of the Gospers Mountain megafire, burning out of control north-west of Sydney in December 2019. This devastating fire season came to be known as Black Summer.

CONTENTS

First Knowledges: An Introduction *Margo Neale*   1

1   Personal Perspectives *Bill Gammage & Bruce Pascoe*   9
2   Land Care *Bruce Pascoe*   20
3   Cultivating Country *Bruce Pascoe*   36
4   Future Farming *Bruce Pascoe*   67
5   Country *Bill Gammage*   75
6   An Ancient Alliance *Bill Gammage*   87
7   Holding the Spark *Bill Gammage*   106
      1788 Fire Notes *Bill Gammage*   128
8   Babes in the Wood *Bill Gammage*   133
9   Poor Fella My Country *Bill Gammage*   152
10   How We Might Love Mother Earth More *Bruce Pascoe*   169

Acknowledgements   186
Image Credits   187
Notes   189
Further Reading   202
Index   203

FIRST KNOWLEDGES

MARGO NEALE, SERIES EDITOR

Country is central to everything Aboriginal: it is a continuum, without beginning or ending. In this worldview, everything is living – people, animals, plants, rocks, earth, water, stars, air and all else. There is no division between animate and inanimate.

Country, sometimes referred to as the Dreaming, holds Law and knowledge. We believe deeply that if you care for Country, Country will care for you. This is the essence of *Country: Future Fire, Future Farming* by Bill Gammage and Bruce Pascoe.

This is the third book in the First Knowledges series of small-format readers – a big title for such compact books. It takes us deep into Country as the previous books did, but differently. This book on caring for Country shows us how to treat and manage Country respectfully in the 21st century, as a matter of urgency for a sustainable future. Nothing could be of more critical contemporary relevance after the fires of 2019–20 and subsequent flood, plague and pandemic events. Indeed, it offers insights into how we can rescue Country from the destructive practices imported by the colonists who, as Bruce Pascoe notes, 'went straight to replicating the systems of the lands they had left, as if they had moved next door, not to another hemisphere'. Instead of learning from the Aboriginal time-tested style of management, which kept this continent healthy and productive for millennia, the colonists created a world where we lurch from one environmental and climatic disaster to another: fire, flood and drought.

The first book in the series, *Songlines: The Power and Promise*, establishes the foundational truths about how all knowledge resides in Country, including medicine, engineering, ecology, kinship systems and social mores. *Design: Building on Country*, the second book, explains the importance of building as an extension of Country and designing spaces as a collaborator, not usurper. It shows how we invest objects made from Country with the spirit of our ancestors. We are now halfway through the First Knowledges series and so well into the discussion – part of a bigger national discourse – about the expertise of First Peoples. *Country: Future Fire, Future Farming* is a call to action for a timely conversation about who we are as Australians on this continent that has been so badly exploited for generations, and about how to take responsibility for its restoration.

Regardless of one's political preference or cultural persuasion, there is momentum building – indeed, a hunger – for greater honesty about this country's past. All bets are off, and all cards are on the table. Part of this is an awareness of the need for a reckoning in this era of truth-telling: the truth about how this continent has been treated – abused, exploited and downtrodden. It follows the divisive history wars – also referred to as the culture wars – that reached their height just after the turn of the century and paved the way to the current demands for truth-telling. While the history wars were fought largely over the reality of the attempted destruction of Aboriginal and Torres Strait Islander people and our removal from recorded history, this new era has seen a widening of the lens to include the destruction of our country, and debates over our sovereignty and a treaty.

The history wars were a war of words, but words have impact and meaning. Was this continent settled or invaded? Were we dispersed or massacred? Were we rescued or removed? Were we removed or stolen? Indeed, were we even human?[1]

Definitions are on the table, too, in this new era. There are varying takes on terms such as 'agriculture' and 'aquaculture', and discussion around whether Aboriginal people were hunter-gatherers or farmers. While both authors of this book acknowledge extensive Aboriginal agency in the farming and gardening of the land, different from the way the misguided colonists farmed and gardened, they diverge on the definition. Bruce takes issue with the hunter-gatherer term as one imposed by the coloniser to denote our primitiveness and lack of civilisation, while Bill chooses to de-primitivise the term and redefine it. He takes it away from the coloniser's intent and instead sees a complex lifestyle where Aboriginal people shaped and mentored the land in collaboration with nature. Bruce, however, cannot accept a definition bestowed on us by Europeans, who were 'at pains to promulgate a hierarchy of humans with themselves at the top', as he puts it. He defines the First Peoples as agriculturalists who did hunt and did gather food (and still do), but who also tilled and harvested the land, manipulated water flows, stored food and gathered seed for redistribution. But the rub was that to be acknowledged as agriculturists by the colonists meant that we would have to be seen as a 'civilised' people, for one equates with the other, and by extension that the land was already occupied and owned. This had significant implications in terms of the notion of terra nullius.

Language is also vital in this current re-engagement with the history of this land and its peoples. It is being energetically contested and examined. Words matter and carry significant meaning. We see this fluid and unsettled space in this series and in this book. Some First Knowledges authors are adamant terms such as Country and Old People should be capitalised as a mark of respect and as recognition of their importance. Others believe these words carry their own weight without capitalisation. Some want to introduce the key historical figures they refer to, but others find descriptions such as 'settlers' not adequate to the truth of those first Europeans they see as invaders. We should be excited by the current renaissance in Indigenous cultures and knowledges. We should embrace these thoughtful debates as necessary and productive.

Country is a myth-buster book. It turns on its head all those falsehoods about Aboriginal people being mere nomads who were at the whim of nature and relied on her bounty for survival, who had no productive interaction with the land and no idea of land management or agriculture. We were, as Bill Gammage describes, 'farmers without fences'. In this book you will learn that for Aboriginal people, fire was our secret weapon, our primary tool used for firestick farming. Fire was a friend, not an enemy. We did not fear fire or use it to reduce fuel load like the newcomers do. We had no fuel overload because of our good land management. The country was shaped with fire by everyone on a regular basis and where necessary. Today we have specialised 'firefighters', but in 1788 everyone was a fire specialist. No corner of this continent was uncared for.

Did you know that there were probably fewer trees here in 1788 than there are today? At the time of invasion, trees were dispersed differently than they are now, and many early colonists described parts of the country as looking like a 'gentleman's park'. Rather than the unmanaged bush full of debris and tangled undergrowth that we see today, there were in some places only an estimated ten to twelve massive trees per acre, and the land was groomed by removing unwanted saplings. Neither were there the dust storms we now experience, where fine topsoils are dumped on cities, denuding the already traumatised land.

The new landlords feared the country, which they regarded as a kind of hostile behemoth that had to be brought to its knees and the elements battled against incessantly. For this, early colonist 'pioneers' were glorified. Conversely, Aboriginal people regarded the continent as a companion in life's journey, a personage to be respected and honoured, loved and nurtured, its power and fragility stewarded. Our people had a give-and-take relationship with Country, or what American philosopher and ecologist David Abram refers to as 'mutualism' in his recognition of a world greater than humans.[2]

For us it is not land, but Country. Country is a worldview that encompasses our relationship to the physical, ancestral and spiritual dimensions, and involves the kind of intimacy evident in the oft-quoted expression 'The Country is our mother. We belong to the country; it does not belong to us.' Indigenous people think of Country as they would a family member. We worry about Country and sing to Country. We care for Country. The rape and pillage of this continent is as abhorrent to us as if it had been done to one's own mother, just to drive home an unsavoury point. It is furthermore immoral to repay the personage who nourishes and nurtures you, who gives you life, with exploitation for greed and short-term gain. The damage of progress is described by Bruce Pascoe, who reminds us that 'The earth is not our collateral, we are hers.'

Throughout the First Knowledges series, we acknowledge the expertise of knowledge holders from both Aboriginal and Western disciplines. This form of co-design or co-authorship in practice is in the spirit of reconciliation, working together interculturally. In *Country*, Bruce writes from an Indigenous perspective on his areas of expertise, which encompass education and farming, while Bill writes from a Western perspective on his areas of expertise across many disciplines, with a focus on history. These authors are like boundary riders as they interrogate old beliefs and present new ways of thinking and doing in their creation of more flexible boundaries.

Both authors are pioneers in their fields and apply traditional knowledges to contemporary circumstances for futuristic ends. Their cultural and individual differences are among the strengths of this book. So are their different stances on many things, including the longevity of human occupation of this continent: one at the current and widely accepted 65,000 years, and the other at the possible but not yet generally accepted 120,000 years. Of course, the date of earliest occupation is continually changing as more of our history is revealed. Knowledge in the Indigenous space is an ever-moving field, dependent on the capacity of Western sciences to 'prove' what the Old People have always known.

While it is clear that colonialism has had an enormous impact on Indigenous societies, this book reveals the other side of that coin: the significant influences that Aboriginal and Torres Strait Islander cultures have had and continue to have on Australian society and history. In many ways, mainstream Australia is only beginning to recognise this. In the process of conveying profound insights into the traditional knowledges of the First Australians, Bill and Bruce illuminate the way forward with a country-centred approach that demands that we look at our continent through Australian eyes and listen to Country and work with her, not against her. They encourage us to learn from Indigenous methods of land management and bring back the native plants that evolved in these ancient soils, including perennials that don't need fertilisers and pesticides or extra water to flourish. They urge us to practise a form of farming that truly responds to the ebb and flow of Country and is powered by old ideas to reinvigorate ancient conversations about the human connection to nature. Here, humans are not at the centre of the dialogue but rather occupy an eco-cultural position such as that championed by David Abram, who learnt from Indigenous peoples. In this way, we can depart the Anthropocene.

To date, little accessible material has been available on Australian Indigenous knowledges for general readers. This series provides a comprehensive and broad range of Indigenous knowledges in one set of accessible, revelatory, hard-to-put-down books – a one-stop shop. It introduces the knowledges of First Australians in ways that are in line with Indigenous ways of knowing and being. It overturns outdated ways of representing – or misrepresenting – Aboriginal and Torres Strait Islander people. Some prevailing assumptions about our culture are challenged and discussed in the series: that Aboriginal people were solely hunters and gatherers, according to primitivist definitions of the terms, but not farmers; that fire is destructive, not a tool for managing the land; that we did not build dwellings and had no technology – despite the sophistication of the boomerang; that we had no knowledge system or history, only myths and legends; that we had no scientists, doctors or lawyers; that we were incapable of innovation. In truth we have a long history as innovators and as peoples who adapted to phenomenal climatic changes, including an ice age and rapid sea-level rise, pestilence and colonisation – and we are still here.

The English language can't effectively describe the many new ideas you will encounter in the First Knowledges series, but we hope the concepts in these books will stimulate and provoke you to enlarge your mind and expand your worldview to encompass limitless other possibilities, including ways in which you can learn from the Aboriginal archive of knowledge embodied in Country.

1

PERSONAL PERSPECTIVES

LITTLE BOOK, BIG STORY

BILL GAMMAGE

I'm delighted to write this book with Bruce Pascoe. He enlarges minds. His listening to and reading of long-available evidence offers fresh insight into the achievement of the people of 1788, and the failure of those who came later to do more than glimpse its scale and grandeur.

For this book we have a specific brief: Bruce to write on plants and animals, me on fire. I suggested and Bruce approved our title, *Country*, but we know that keeping only to plants, animals and fire omits much essential to Country as a philosophical and emotional understanding of how places, people, plants and animals share responsibility for the harmony and continuity of existence.

But help is at hand. The first book in the First Knowledges series, Margo Neale and Lynne Kelly's *Songlines*, explains Songlines and their expression on the ground and in paint, song, dance and story. These are essential elements of Country, and no doubt later books in the series will add more.

Much of my writing here stems from work for my book *The Biggest Estate on Earth: How Aborigines Made Australia*. On many aspects that book is heavy with evidence, freeing me to tread lightly here. This might reverse the balance of two common responses to *The Biggest Estate*: some readers will think I offer too much evidence, and others too little.

There are four ground-floor changes from that book.

1. In reporting fire in the Centre and north, this book is more likely to use recent examples. In those regions I see continuity from 1788, while this book has more on fire after 1788 than did *The Biggest Estate*. One consequence is that the tense I use flips between past and present. In those cases I am arguing or accepting that what is so now was essentially so then.
2. In discussing fire in *The Biggest Estate* I took 'no fire' – deliberately not burning – as its obvious corollary, and I assumed readers would too. My mistake. I correct this with a note on no fire in opening Chapter 5.
3. *The Biggest Estate* and my talks since rank fuel reduction as the basic 1788 fire, the necessary preliminary to every other

fire type. My mistake again. Joe Morrison, Group CEO of the Indigenous Land and Sea Corporation, pointed out, 'Reduced fuel is an outcome of why people burn. Fuel reduction was not an end in itself, but a colonial paradigm in which fire is seen as ultimately bad and associated with evil, not renewal, rebirth and as good.'[1] Fuel reduction fire was never necessary because other fires regulated fuel anyway. Only after 1788 did whitefella neglect spur fuel reduction to prominence. I have upended my earlier accounts of fuel reduction fire.

4. A caution about 'management'. The word is entrenched, and I use it. Yet it downplays 1788's necessary ceremonial envelope, and it is hierarchical – people manage, the rest are managed. 'Care' is closer to 1788, but it too assumes hierarchy. In 1788 people thought more of collaboration. All creation shared responsibility for maintaining the universe. This was the point of ceremony. Ceremony voices one of 1788's great intellectual achievements – to assert the interdependence of life and things. Trying to understand 1788 in simply Western terms is folly. It lets some researchers say in effect, 'We can't see why or how Aborigines did x or y, so they didn't.' They think like managers. Be warned.

BELIEVING IN GOD, ACTING LIKE THE DEVIL

BRUCE PASCOE

The past two years have shaken our assumed ability to control nature. We should reflect on our impact on the world and our attempts to assert dominance and pursue more conservative land management and more modest demands on soil, water and air. If the world is determined to have this massive and increasing population, then we might only survive by modifying our wasteful lifestyles.

There are commercial opportunities in changing our approach to land use and consumption. To change is not an abnegation of capitalism but a repudiation of its dangerous profligacy. We can keep our computers and mobile phones as long as we recycle their components, we can keep our washing machines and fridges as long as their parts are recyclable, and we can afford to power all of them as long as we use sustainable power. We do not need to throw babies and bathwater all over the geraniums in order to have a more sustainable world.

Advances in medical science are responsible for our dangerously high population, but a few well-planned social reforms can redress that issue. For example, smaller families across the globe can help raise living standards in the developing world. To suggest measures of restraint in the developed world is not class warfare but the application of decency.

My family has benefited directly from modern science, so I am not one to suggest we all need to don sackcloth and dust ourselves with ashes. Changing behaviour doesn't mean abandonment of all that is useful. Fifty-five years of right-arm medium-pace bowling reduced my left hip to a degenerate EH Holden brake disc pad, scooped and dysfunctional. I had a replacement performed by a surgeon going by the disconcerting name of 'Crayfish'. The anaesthetic was so light and acutely graduated that I woke towards the end of the operation and looked up to see the Crayfish talking to someone. His apprentice. The trainee was hammering a 5000-dollar stainless steel device with what looked like Uncle Alan's wooden mallet. I wish I hadn't seen that, but I am eternally grateful for the medical science and engineering that allowed me to play another decade of cricket, to swim, to climb mountains, to jump into my boat.

My mother had a seizure due to her epilepsy and a large clot formed on her brain. We lived on King Island. She was flown to Melbourne by Brain & Brown's geriatric airline. It was early days in cranial pressure relief and later, my father asserted, he could have done the operation himself for half the price with his own brace and bit.

My mother prospered and, thanks to the surgeon, went on to win gold medals for Australia in the Paralympics. She was grateful too, but then Mum was grateful for everything her God gave her. I had long ago stopped believing in her God but was deeply appreciative of her survival because she hadn't stopped teaching me about grace, beauty and goodness. I was nowhere near the top student in her class, but I'll never forget her love and greatness of mind.

So, my family has many reasons to be grateful to science and respectful of its ability to help humans. But we don't have to approve of everything it does. I'm not sure the Crayfish approved of the bomb that destroyed Nagasaki; I'm certain Mum's surgeon would have deplored Agent Orange. There are some things about modern science, engineering and industry that we could do without. Built-in obsolescence and the cascading range of automobiles from a plethora of companies seems an extreme adherence to the market system. Some innovations are generated by that competition, but the price of waste and excessive resource use must be where a mature economic system has responsibility for change. Plastic electric toothbrushes, disposable televisions, disposable nappies, disposable serviettes and dental floss apparati are things a world determined to conserve itself cannot afford.

We can modify the market economy and not threaten to create a communist state. Democracies should be flexible and honourable enough to act reasonably and caringly without the need for street demonstrations against a languishing state. Some claim this is hoping for too much from the human spirit, but I think an example of innovation and ingenuity without waste or damage to Mother Earth is right here under our noses. It is common for Australians to look elsewhere for spiritual enlightenment: we float lilies on other people's sacred pools, climb the steps of ancient temples, pray in churches because they happen to be in Paris or Rome, but we have rarely chosen to examine the spirituality and philosophy of the world's oldest continuing and most sustainable culture – here, Australia.

I receive plenty of electronic invective abusing me for gilding the black lily, but what I ask is that we consider this ancient and successful civilisation as a necessary part of any future analysis of human survival. There are many aspects of modern life where simple respect for the earth could be a successful investment in our combined future.

The modern industrial state can mine where we could never mine before, but seemingly cannot prevent its tailings dams from collapsing and drowning thousands of people in sludge and poisoning the environment for a thousand years. We can mine ores and render them into metals to clad spacecraft but cannot prevent the miner from exploding a cave of 46,000-year-old art.[2] Why? The public acquiesces so easily to the demands for progress regardless of the cost to our common wealth. In the case of that art gallery, the mineral involved is so common that the need to mine anywhere within a bull's roar of the cave was negligible. The fact of doing so, contempt.

This demand for exploitation debases the meaning of the word 'progress'. Polluting a river, destroying the ozone layer and seeding the ocean with plastic fragments that eliminate whole species of fish should not be seen as collateral damage but as a signal that our methods of production cannot be tolerated if we wish to hand over the globe to our grandchildren in such a state that they may prosper.

———

When the Industrial Revolution began, the European mind devised laws to eliminate the rural peasantry and convert them into factory slaves; the workhouse.[3] The old system of landed peasantry was abolished so that a class of incredibly wealthy people could eat larks' tongues and saffron. This is not innovation, it is an aberration and ought to be repulsed by our religions.

Those convicts and migrants who rode on the heels of the Australian invasion were children of that thought process and, dismissing the local population to feed their ambition for wealth, they used brutal methods of land clearance.[4] The effect of sheep and cattle is recognised,[5] but in the east-coast tropical forests and the wet sclerophylls of southern Australia the aggression and greed were breathtaking.

At Byron Bay great forests of cedar trees covered the ranges right down to the beaches but such was the unrestrained avarice and rapine that every tree had been felled within decades. The book *Red Gold* by John Vader[6] speaks in awe of the energy and ingenuity of the cedar getters. Many Australian history books are like this, breathless and genuflectic to the brave explorer and the indomitable miner, forester, squatter and, like *Red Gold*, they never mention Aboriginal people or the invasion, just as a second-hand car dealer never mentions the banana skin in the wonky gearbox that will get you only far enough away from the car yard that you can't come back.

The energy of those early entrepreneurs cannot be denied, but their short-term business plan, 'how much can I get before it's all gone', has to be deplored.

Where the terrain was more difficult or where the absence of cedars made the forest of less interest to Europeans, the cheapest way to 'clear' the land was to destroy the forest entirely. In the books *Green Mountains* by Bernard O'Reilly and *The Bush* by Don Watson,[7] the methods used are explained in appalling detail. The trees of a mountain slope were scarfed, deeply notched with an axe on the downhill side, and then the trees on the ridge were felled onto those below so that the whole forest cascaded onto itself like dominoes, like the dominion the Bible endorsed.[8] The forest became a million split and tangled skewers. The timber was impossible to salvage and so the whole thing was burnt. Soils that had not been exposed for a million years were naked.

Find an eight-year-old and, when they have finished fixing your computer, ask them this question: What do you think will happen next time there is heavy rain in such an area? The child will not even need to know the annual average rainfall of the region; they will tell you that the soil will plummet from the hillsides in a slurry that will render once-navigable deep-water streams into sterile puddles.

Why were these 'farmers', these 'husbands of the soil' surprised when the land they had 'cleared' was immediately devoid of its topsoil? The kid will be asking you that question. It was carnage, the profligate enterprise of vandals, with no adult willing to raise a voice against the destruction. This stupidity should never have been tolerated in a Christian heart. We should be using this example as a caution to every agriculture and business studies student. Just because there is a resource does not mean it must be expended in one individual's lifetime.

Our misuse of resources is not limited to the soil. The orange roughy, a fish discovered by commercial fisheries in the 1980s, was all but eliminated by overfishing in only a few years. The fish can live to be 140 years of age. They congregate for breeding in great columns in the Southern Ocean and when commercial fishers discovered this phenomenon, they plundered the columns again and again. This didn't just interrupt the breeding but brought the species to the point of obliteration.[9]

When the Australian cedar getters were eliminating red cedars from the eastern forests, where was the government? When fishers bring many species to the point of extinction, where is the public's rebuke? Our business schools must ensure that such craven overuse of resources is never extolled as world's best practice. Our next generation should be made to embrace true conservatism in relation to resources they never own. That is smart business.

The European business impulse seems to rely on the right of capitalism to completely expend a resource; if companies do not have this right, advocates of the model say, the laissez-faire principle will collapse. The right of men, yes I mean men, to plunder a resource to the total expenditure of the capital must be reined in. It should be anathema to young men to entirely destroy a resource that is owned by the world. There must have been a time when it was possible for wise heads in industry to say, 'Sufficient profit has been made from the cedar. Now we must conserve the last forests for the sake of our grandchildren.' And what would a forest of those trees be worth to the tourism industry today?

There were attempts to grow plantations of red cedar after the forests were gone but they were thwarted by the cedar tip moth, which ate the growing tips of the trees and left them stunted and undeveloped.[10] The planters scratched their heads in frustration but it was the engine of capital accumulation that was their enemy, not the insect. When the forest was destroyed, so were the birds, insects and animals that kept it in environmental health. We may never know how many species became extinct when their home was removed.

We must insist that capitalism provides us with a true business model to show that enterprise is capable of providing more than a Maserati for two generations of a business family. There must be a plan for a product's future beyond the aggrandisement of one ego-driven male. We must build into our business models the idea of true conservatism so that we place a value on the earth itself rather than succumb to the idea that business is an excuse for wanton vandalism.

2

LAND CARE

Europeans had an uncomfortable relationship with this continent. The invaders saw the land as savage and aggressive to humans. It had to be fought into submission. Its spiders, sharks and snakes were lying in wait to get you. It had to be conquered because it refused to be England.

Did this attitude creep into the people's psyche because of the nature of the land or because of our tenuous claim to legitimacy? Were we unconsciously deflecting guilt of our invasion by condemning the land as our enemy?

That dread of the continent was reflected onto the ancient forests and developed into antipathy. Men began to think of trees as enemies, the best use for which was to adorn their pride and fortune. This might stretch back to the time when the lighthouse at Alexandria was built to guide ships so commerce would not be hampered by mere geography and the fall of night. That commercial imperative denuded Arabia of its forest, and the proliferation of goats, and that animal's preference for seedling trees,[1] ensured it could never return.

Or did this careless antipathy begin in 1250, when people on Easter Island carved ever bigger moai from stone to intimidate their enemies; that is, their cousins and fellow humans. These massive figures had to be moved into position by using the trunks of cut trees as rollers. Celebrating their ego resulted in a man standing beneath the last tree and wondering, 'Will I cut this last tree to satisfy my hatred of my cousin, or will I save it for my grandchildren and for the sake of trees themselves? No, I'll cut it down – my hatred needs more satisfaction than the mere existence of a tree.'

Exactly when this idea occurred in the human brain is not important but the result was that people and their religions and commerce began to see the natural world as their dominion. Our forests, oceans and soils are dangerously diminished as a direct consequence of that assumption of humans' position in relation to their home. The male commercial ego and religions which declare the world as the dominion of humans are the cause of almost all wars and global environmental destruction.

It took a mob of reviled hippies to save whales from complete destruction in the 1970s and 80s,[2] but that selflessness now allows millionaires to run whale tours. But who will save the trees? Will we leave that responsibility to hippies, or will we do the heavy lifting ourselves, as conservative politicians like to say, as if only they can do real work.

The east-coast fires during the summer of 2019–20 were accelerated in the forests created to feed the woodchip mills. The layout of commercial forests means that a large number of same-size trees are grown in close proximity, often no more than 2 metres apart, which ensures quick fire spread into the crown. In combination with high fuel loads in unkempt national parks, the forests of small silvertop ash were guaranteed to turn a fire into an inferno. Nothing could be done to prevent it.

These small-tree forests were created by repeated logging over the last 230 years and have allowed us to believe that what we now see, crowded and tangled commercial forests and national parks, is the real Australian wilderness. But the old Aboriginal forest of ten to twelve massive trees to the acre[3] has largely disappeared. The demand for paper and packaging has turned our forests into a commodity, and the failure to keep the forest understorey controlled has meant that we are now in danger when we live anywhere near a commercial plantation. We need to staff and maintain national parks with a view to safety and care, and our forests must be managed so that Australia gets both economic and environmental benefit from them, not just a quick injection of funds to large companies in a fire sale of national assets.

Aboriginal people had a burning regime that produced fewer but bigger trees. The crowns of these massive trees were never in contact and forests were maintained as places to grow grass and vegetables, graze game animals and make travel comfortable for humans (see Chapter 5). Fire in such forests is controllable.

When the 2019–20 fires had abated near Mallacoota, in Victoria, my neighbours and I cut our way back along the roads that led to our farms and houses to fight the more localised fires still threatening us. While we were busy, contractors moved in behind us and painted a 'K' on almost every big tree at the roadside, whether it threatened to collapse onto the road or not.[4] K for killer. The 'K' didn't mean killer fire, or killer forestry, or killer forest management, but killer tree. The trees were to blame. One of our local foresters bought cans of black spray paint and desperately tried to hide all the insidious Ks. Our lone hero did his best, but thousands of grand trees were destroyed to keep the contractors happy.

The most ancient trees seemed to bear the brunt of this system, including several scar trees and one where my uncle was made to sleep to prove to his grandfather that he was ready for the lore. That tree was massive, and the atrium at its base was large enough for two people to sleep comfortably. It had five large windows in the trunk that had been made by Dooligah to express the power of the lore. People today are frightened of Dooligah, but he only upholds the lore, he is not an instrument of casual violence. That was the old grandfather's message: uphold your lore. We begged Parks Victoria to look out for this tree a year before the fires exploded, but in the aftermath the Dooligah tree was cut down. It didn't burn, couldn't have burnt, but it was cut down and other trees were felled on top of it because they were also 'killer' trees.

Recently one of our Yuin horticulturalists found a large felled tree displayed in an Eden logging company's yard. It had been one of the old people's ring trees, deliberately manipulated to form an oval 10 metres long. That tree in situ has an invaluable cultural role but cut down and displayed, all it shows is how little Australia cares for its history.

We need to use Australia's forests to sustain our communities. Our forests have done that for around 120,000 years, as evidenced by soil cores, which are used to analyse human use of fire,[5] but we need to manage and value them differently. We need fewer but larger trees per acre. We need to harvest trees for timber but maximise the use of that timber and enhance its value. We need to respect the trees we harvest by paying for their true value. At the moment we clear-fell entire forests and leave the forest floor as a ruin of stumps and gouged soil; and then we wonder why the next crop of plantation timber is more spindly than the one before it. We turn the perfect timber into woodchips, send it to Japan for processing and then buy it back as packaging for our hamburgers. Industry is manipulating our governance to gain access to our common wealth, but if we want to have forests for our grandchildren we, as a community, need to manage all usage. I am not talking about closing forests so that bushwalkers can experience 'wilderness', but managing and caring for forests in order to keep both them and the community safe.

There are few wilderness forests in Australia. Wilderness was a concept unknown to Aboriginal people prior to 1788: they visited and used every corner of the land and were in intimate communication with it. Our later colonial writings and songs are all about hardship and the antipathy of the land to the invaders, rarely about love and beauty. The accounts and paintings of the early European explorers described the land they saw at the beginning of the invasion as verdant and open, pleasant and gentle. Large trees dominated a landscape that was interspersed with rich grasslands and tuber fields. There were no fences, apart from those used for game drives, because the land didn't belong to individuals; it was bestowed on language groups and clans so that they would care for it, not exploit it.

The land's appearance was a result of the continuous use of controlled fire by Aboriginal and Torres Strait Islander people to remove unwanted brush and saplings.[6] As my co-author, Bill Gammage, states in Chapter 6, 'people ... thinned or cleared trees for grass [and] removed scrub to open an understorey'. The elimination of unwanted saplings enabled the crops to prosper. Cool fires were a tool of management.

Preventing the high level of Aboriginal land management allowed the scrub to encroach on all areas not actually tilled by European ploughs, and gradually Australians began to see tangled undergrowth as normal. Timber operations to supply sleepers for Indian and Australian railways removed the larger trees and encouraged more scrub to grow until this new bush was considered natural.[7]

The volatility of the undergrowth that appeared after colonisation allowed a quick point of ignition, and its height allowed flames to reach into the first branches of the larger trees. Our fear of fire began and was soon heightened by massive wildfires that swept through the crowded forests and into towns and suburbs.

The newcomers' failure to accept that the country they had invaded had been carefully managed for many thousands of years meant that important indicators of danger were missed. Later generations saw the dangers as symptomatic of a hostile land, preventing us from correcting the encroachment of undergrowth. Australian art and literature emphasised our fear of the land and its hostility towards us. It was a desert, it had spiders, sharks and snakes. These creatures loomed large in the consciousness and media of the nation. Australians are taught to fear the country and so we cluster on the coast and fail to implement the forest care that would make the country safer for all of us.

———

Before the eastern-seaboard fires of 2019–20, residents and fire crews had been anticipating a horrible fire season but it eventuated in a far worse form than anyone had seen before. Those of us who live in this part of Australia experienced psychological trauma during that summer, and afterwards we were exhausted. To venture into the forest to watch the recovery was gruelling as it meant returning to places we'd left feeling despair, fear and bone-weariness. Many residents left the region altogether, too horrified and disappointed to remain, and too many others left because they had lost their homes.

On the Wallagaraugh River we were spared the massive assault of hot air and ash that exploded on Mallacoota and Cobargo and towns all along Australia's east coast. Instead, we had repeated approaches from the fire as it surged through the forests at the whim of the winds. Most of the time it came slowly, but occasionally it rolled across our paddocks like huge barrels of fire. Mostly we could contain it with firebreaks and hoses, but sometimes we retreated to our verandahs and wondered if we'd see the same table and teacups the next day.

We have a number of people from the local Aboriginal community working on our far East Gippsland farm, Yumburra, and we've put a lot of work into growing ancestral grasses and tubers so that our people will have a stake in the Aboriginal food market. This is an important step in the new industry of growing Aboriginal foods, because of all the money made out of these foods only 1 per cent ends up with Aboriginal people.[8] We want to participate in the industry so that, should we be brought to court again over our right to pursue our culture on our land, we will not be told, as the Yorta Yorta were, that our culture was 'washed away by the tide of history'.[9]

In the aftermath of the fires, Mother Earth invited us into the forest and insisted that we observe her recovery, her power. The tree ferns were first, generating celebratory, bright-green fanfares of promise against a background of ash and char where the giant spars of fallen trees were like a graveyard for burnt galleons. Rushes thrust up spears of electric green and then epicormic shoots appeared on the eucalypts; bronze, pink and vermilion flames licked at the blackened trunks. Later the wattles and kangaroo apples sprang up from seed they had cast after the blaze.

The vivid response revived us a little and we went looking for seedlings. The forest floor was studded with emergent green: ironbarks, peppermints, hickory wattles, casuarinas, cherries and brave maidenhairs. We wanted to use these seedlings to rebuild burnt areas and enhance others, and as we lifted and potted plants our spirits rebounded a little. When we combed our croplands to study the species' recovery we were charmed and exhilarated to find apple berry, glycines and lomandras and stunned to see so many orchids where we had never seen them before. We had removed cattle from Yumburra two seasons earlier in order to rest and revive the soil and then the fires suppressed some common weeds, which allowed our own fire-resistant plants to flourish. The leek orchids were lush and plump and we marvelled at the revelation of what a fire and the removal of hard-hoofed animals could do.

Those fires also burnt our crop of kangaroo grass and it felt like a year of work had been in vain. I felt devastated for the community, but only weeks later, and with the benefit of a good rain, the grasses were back and booming without competition from the exotics. We were able to harvest two different grasses, mamadyang ngalluk and garrara ngalluk, in June 2020, and by the end of the year we also had buru ngalluk prospering. It was remarkable to see tall grasses coming back, not just at the edge of the forest but deep inside it. We had seen some examples of garrara ngalluk on roadsides but by November it was dominant at the edge of the forest, and within the forest it was growing strongly. This was a surprise as we'd never seen it under the trees before. The canopy of the bigger trees had been eliminated by the fire and so plants we didn't recognise as forest plants were flourishing. We also found a lot of manjamanja ngalluk. All of these grasses were used by our old people to produce flour.

The presence of all these plants growing in the forest after the fires provided us with an opportunity to re-examine our land use. This type of growth is what the first 'explorers and pioneers' observed and what Bill Gammage outlined in *The Biggest Estate on Earth*. Australian colonists ignored the First Peoples' style of management and went straight to replicating the systems of the lands they had left, as if they had moved next door, not to another hemisphere. They began ploughing soil and planting exotic food plants, and almost completely ended the use of fire in the landscape.

We need to change our thinking about how to farm the country. Aboriginal people managed and harvested these lands in common. When farmers began to use tractors directed by satellite navigation about thirty years ago, they pulled down fences between properties so that the huge machines could harvest in straight lines over hundreds of kilometres, twenty-four hours a day. It was an economically rational idea. We may not be able to replicate the ancient common wealth, but perhaps new methods and new crops will allow us to do more things in common and with less machinery, fuel and soil compaction.

The fires of 2019–20 gave us a little clue to the alternative. Harvesting between trees is not what our monocultural system believes in, but having a forest and food on the same land provides an opportunity to reassess forest management. Since the cessation of regular applications of cool fire (see Chapter 3), Australians have argued about fuel loads and mismanagement. Not all forests will be suitable as food forests and this can be gauged from the fact that before 1788, Aboriginal people chose to work the more manageable slopes and temperate forests.

Conservationists need not fear that all nesting sites and diversity will be lost, as this type of forest nurtured the diversity that the colonists encountered on their entry into the country. For example, bandicoots and potoroos were abundant in the precolonial forest but have all but disappeared due to our subsequent land use and the presence of cats and foxes. We now know that bandicoots are crucial to soil health because they assist the spread of mycorrhizal fungi and aerate the ground more deeply.[10] They are adapted to grasslands in open forest and we miss their contributions to our soil health.

Australia seems to lurch from one farming crisis to another. Drought relief costs our government millions when the answer might be growing plants that are less water-hungry. We despair when blue-green algae and fish kills in the Murray-Darling Basin become national news every summer, but that nightmare might be eradicated by moving away from crops like rice and cotton, which require the most water and for which our government has allowed the massive enclosure of the northern river catchments for the creation of private dams.[11] The management solution the government thought to apply was to privatise the national water supply, but that system has failed to deliver either sufficient environmental flows to keep fish alive or enough to maintain the profits of downstream farms.[12] Land use has to be revisited for the sake of those farms and the whole country. All parts of Australia are threatened by the failure to understand the very nature of Australian soils.

We don't need to adopt all Aboriginal methods, but in this time of water, soil and farm-income crisis, it would seem a prudent management approach to consider the condition of the country at the time of the invasion. This condition was produced by a people who had up to 120,000 years of experience on the continent[13] and a spirituality that always put the land first.

I take the age of occupation as 120,000 years from Gurdip Singh's research at Lake George in New South Wales a few decades ago and Jim Bowler's Moyjil/Point Ritchie research in south-west Victoria, concluded and peer reviewed two years ago. This age is contentious, as all major shifts in knowledge must be, but I am assuming the science to be correct. Our people say that we have always been here, a claim many believe to be metaphorical, but in terms of the longevity of other world civilisations maybe 120,000 years is 'all of time'. Many of the knowledges expressed in Aboriginal story suggest experience of the continent much earlier than 120,000 years.

Sceptics who cannot abide the thought of any Aboriginal achievement will ridicule our efforts, but their philosophies have bankrupted our soil. Whether this is because of antipathy to the very idea of Aboriginal competence or dedication to a mantra learnt in Australian schools and perpetuated by parliament and society is sometimes difficult to tell. Anthropologist Peter Sutton quoted Captain John Hunter of the First Fleet to debunk the idea of Aboriginal cultivation because he talked about the 'wild' yams the natives were eating.[14] Hunter's use of the word wild is meant to decry any intent of production by Aboriginal people, but it is just the sort of word an Englishman in his first days in the colony would use.

Other colonists in many different areas of Australia described the enormous effort expended by the First Peoples to grow, cultivate, harvest and maintain crops of tubers, grasses and other plant foods as well as meat animals and fish.[15]

Sometimes opposition to any idea of Aboriginal engagement in the landscape borders on hysteria. Where is the problem in accepting the reality that so many colonists described? Those sceptical of Aboriginal agricultural management insist that Aboriginal people were simply taking advantage of the natural order and accuse me of deploring the idea of the hunter-gatherer. Aboriginal and Torres Strait Islander people did hunt and did gather and still do today, but we also tilled, harvested, manipulated water flows across the land, and stored food. Aboriginal people were known to select seed and carry it in small conical baskets suspended from their necks so that they could trade or gift it to neighbouring clans. Recent archaeology is proving that palms, tubers and grasses were distributed widely across Australia by Aboriginal agency.[16] We were not innocent of interaction with the continent.

Some Aboriginal people have become so wedded to the idea that we were hunters and gatherers that evidence to the contrary is ignored. But why should we accept a definition bestowed on us by Europeans who were at pains to promulgate a hierarchy of humans with themselves at the top? Of course, Hunter would call Aboriginal food plants 'wild'. The very act of choosing seed and resowing in suitable new country is what agricultural scientists know as agriculture. 'Civilisation' and 'agriculture' are considered by many European scholars to have evolved together. Storage of seed, water control, organised harvest and housing are the major characteristics of an agricultural economy. Australia was thought to fall short of these tests, but Rupert Gerritsen, in his book *Australia and the Origins of Agriculture*, provides extensive evidence to the contrary.[17] My book *Dark Emu* relies heavily on Gerritsen's work.

Peter Sutton and archaeologist Keryn Walshe have recently released a book criticising *Dark Emu* for not respecting the hunter-gatherer system of the First Australians.[18] Hunting and gathering is a sustainable and healthy lifestyle but it is not the only thing Aboriginal and Torres Strait Islander people did. We also farmed and gardened, not in the same way as Europeans, but why should we? This is a different continent.

Some academics seem confronted by the idea that Aboriginal people refused to follow all the behaviours of hunter-gatherer peoples. The word 'domestication' seems to be a red rag to these bulls of history, but domestication occurs when humans harvest fruits or seeds of plants in a systematic pattern over a period of years. If you conduct that system over thousands and thousands of years, the changes to the plant genome are profound.

Aboriginal people were prevented from continuing their land management because massacres and stray killings depleted the workforce and it became too dangerous for them to venture out in the open. This level of murder and intimidation is well documented in all states and lasted well into the 20th century.[19] It was horrible to see in *The Guardian* in March 2021 a photograph of Aboriginal men chained by the neck for resisting the law of the invaders. They were chained to a tree and left out in the sun for days. These chains were still being used in 1958, two years after the Melbourne Olympics.[20]

At Yumburra we were thrilled to see indigenous grasses come back to the forest. It vindicates our decision to try to return the forest on our farm to one where big trees and food grasses dominate. This doesn't mean we will lose our wattles and grevilleas, indigoferas and hakeas: the biodiversity will remain, but we'll end up with a productive and far less flammable forest. We intend to remove the smaller eucalypts from our farm's forest lands and sell the timber as sawlogs. Already we have used a lot of this timber to build fences and sheds on the farm. It's a slow process and won't be achieved overnight, but we are trying to reverse the poor land-management decisions of the last 230 years.

We are experimenting with an adaptation of our harvester so that we can harvest grasses within the forest, not just in open country. If we are successful, it may provide us with an opportunity to change the idea of how to farm this continent. We are fortunate to have an Aboriginal engineer and steel fabricator in our community and hope that after we have designed our next, bigger harvester, he will build it for us and we can also begin to reverse the horrible statistics of Aboriginal inclusion in the agricultural industry.[21]

Aboriginal agency in the landscape has legal implications because a treaty for the land has never been negotiated. We must also consider that it has environmental and economic implications, both of which are positive for our common wealth. If we can acclimatise ourselves to the real history of the country and the real land-use practices of Aboriginal people, we can open ourselves to positions of advantage.

Australians have found it very difficult to include Aboriginal people in any national debate, but overcoming this reticence and recognising national Aboriginal land management will free us from the mistakes we have made in the past and allow us to contemplate an agriculture and conservation suitable for this continent, not one in the Northern Hemisphere.

There are still people who are scornful of the evidence of Aboriginal accomplishment, but 120,000 years of prosperous forest management might one day be seen as genius. That management system has to be part of our response to current agricultural and environmental dangers. Big businesses in the forest industry will heap ridicule on the idea and find plenty of social media trolls to do their bidding, but it is our forest and we must pay attention to its needs. Proper care will serve our economy well and we will still have forests to serve as balm for our burnt souls.

I am sure that people who love the bush in its present state will learn to love a more open and less combustible pre-1788 style of forest. All the birds, insects and animals will still be there, but the koalas and wallabies will never have their pads burnt off in uncontrolled fire. It will be a different forest from the one we see today, but Australia has experienced this forest type before, during the eons of Aboriginal forest management.

3

CULTIVATING COUNTRY

If we are to going to return forests to a condition in which we can live more safely, that is, the condition of the old Aboriginal forest, we should learn about the nutritional qualities of that forest. Permaculturalists are asking us to consider the merits of refining the monocultures of European-style industrial farming.[1] More diversity encourages chemically positive interactions between plants, and the use of fewer chemical fertilisers leads to healthier soils.

Australian soils are relatively low in nutrients as a result of being so old compared to most soils in the world. They need fertiliser to grow exotic plants but need nothing to grow ours. They are perfect as they are. Our plants have had millions of years to adapt to low soil fertility. We need to use this fact to our advantage rather than try to change history by adding chemical fertilisers. Grow Australian plants in Australia, that's pocket science.

Using the bush as a source of food has many benefits. There are challenges in harvesting these diverse plants in a woodland setting, but the production inputs are nil, so there is an economic logic in examining a new farming model. The biggest problem for Australia is to acknowledge the intellectual property Aboriginal people have in these plants. Demand for the produce is guaranteed. Restaurants and wholefood stores are clamouring for the food, but very few have any idea how to include Aboriginal people in the benefits of foods that have been domesticated by Aboriginal people.

A plant becomes domesticated after it has been harvested continuously over many years. The plant begins to adapt to human interaction. The Australian food plants we see today have a commercial and cultural connection to Aboriginal and Torres Strait Islander people. Australia's superficial knowledge of Aboriginal history, and in particular agricultural history, means that it is rare for us to consider the debt owed to tens of thousands of years of land management. The biodiversity Europeans encountered on entry into the country was created by the management of Aboriginal people. We need to look at our country differently, acknowledge the wealth of Aboriginal plant, environment and economic skills, and adopt different techniques, even if they call into question the methods imported from Europe.

Thinking differently about land use will neither destroy the environment nor flummox our souls. Treating the land with more thought for her dignity will not undermine our commerce. Greater care of the resource is likely to improve it. There is a 120,000-year history of agriculture and horticulture in the country, and to ignore such a vast body of knowledge would seem churlish at best and economic madness at worst.

The challenge for Australia is to go beyond a warm and fuzzy enthusiasm for eating Aboriginal foods. We must move towards a stern insistence that land and social justice be extended to Aboriginal and Torres Strait Islander people before we accept the commercial and environmental advantages these foods offer. Growing more perennial food plants is going to be wonderful for our land, and for meeting our carbon emission reduction targets, but to accept these gifts without recompense to the people who domesticated them is just another dispossession. You can't eat our food if you can't swallow our history.

At Yumburra, Black Duck Foods[2] grows the traditional perennial foods of the region and employs Aboriginal people in the agriculture. The aim is to demonstrate to other Aboriginal communities that we can grow the foods, find a market for them and give employment to our own people. We have already developed a recipe to make a pesto using our warrigal greens and a preserved samphire, plants that we simply pick from our paddocks and swamp verges. Our grains are being converted into flour so that we can bake a variety of breads, and these have been received enthusiastically by some of the top chefs in Australia. When we bought the farm the river flats were stark, but once the cattle were removed a whole host of useful vegetables returned. There are pasture weeds as well, but with judicious use of fire we are managing to control those.

Many Aboriginal and Torres Strait Islander plants have commercial and culinary potential, and those I talk about in this chapter are just a few. The plants here are those with which I have direct experience, but a similar array of useful plants could be compiled for any Australian region. For example, forms of kangaroo grass appear right across the country.

CUMBUNGI (OR NGURUN) AND WATER RIBBON

Early European entrants to country reported on the fecundity of the regions of Australia where they travelled. Even interior regions that today are described as desert had tall grasses, and the ephemeral lake beds were lush with nardoo or murnong.

Lieutenant George Grey in Western Australia found himself among warran (yam) grounds that extended beyond the horizon in every direction.[3] Thomas Mitchell rode through 9 miles (14.5 kilometres) of ricked grain around the Barwon River in the New South Wales/Queensland border region.[4] The hillsides of Melbourne were terraced by Aboriginal people in the production of yam.[5]

These examples of rich productivity were rarely attributed to Aboriginal endeavour by the early colonists, but some, including Edward Curr, James Kirby, Peter Beveridge, Isaac Batey and others, wrote extensively of their early observations.[6] They grudgingly admitted the beauty of the country and the skill of Aboriginal land management but almost always fell back on aphorisms about the superiority of their own land-use techniques. When we compare those early observations of soil health to the eroded, salinated and compacted soils of today, we become aware of the refinement of Aboriginal methods of soil management.

Kirby and Beveridge rode through an area of marshy country to the south of Swan Hill in north-west Victoria and were bemused by the steaming mounds of cumbungi leaves they saw.[7] The mounds were as high as a house and were stacked for the purpose of food and fibre extraction. We don't know if a fire was lit below to produce the heat or whether the heat was generated by such a dense pile of plant material. The starch from the leaves was collected in order to make flour, and the base of the plant is probably the loveliest salad vegetable I have ever eaten. There will be a market for the flour, fibre and vegetable of this plant, but at the moment farmers are spending millions dredging it from canals or eliminating it altogether in the process of draining swamps.

The Macquarie marshes in north-western New South Wales, where a large national park was created in 1971, are an abundant source of cumbungi. These marshes were managed by Aboriginal people as an economic and environmental zone before invasion and so, by fencing them off, we are corralling a very important food source. The local Wailwan people periodically burnt the marshes in a mosaic to rejuvenate growth but in a way that allowed animals to relocate safely. Once again, we might need to look at how we see a national park and how we see a farm. Perhaps in some cases they might be the same area. That will be a huge shift in how we relate to our country, but given the plight of the world's environment such shifts, while difficult, are becoming necessary.

The water ribbon is another plant used by Aboriginal people for food and fibre. The tuber is delicious but our systems of irrigation and channel clearance destroy vast amounts of this useful plant.

Both cumbungi and water ribbon are incredibly important for water filtration. It is possible to witness this capability during modern channel clearance operations. Where an excavator is working to tear the cumbungi or water ribbon from the channel or stream, the water is a muddy slough, but downstream of the works the water emerges from the still-standing vegetation as clear.

Cattle plunder water ribbon and cumbungi when they find it, selecting these plants for their nutritional benefits. What if we excluded cattle from the waterways so that the plants could prosper, and utilised the produce as a natural part of our agricultural economy?

We are experimenting with both of these crops at Yumburra by working with knowledge retained in the community and information we can glean from the public record. It is a slow process, and aggravating that so much knowledge was lost during the frontier period and the subsequent introduction of swamp clearance.

That ignorance and vandalism continues. For example, Byron Bay Shire wants to create 350 new blocks of land by building a 6-metre-high wall to enable a swamp to be filled with rubble and soil. Regardless of the need for housing, where is the consideration for the integrity of a drainage system and the wildlife refuge it represents? The white shoe brigade is alive and well. We need all levels of government to insist on the highest standards of protection for our remaining wetlands.

A wetland was returned to health in Warrnambool, Victoria, a couple of years after a group of factories was closed down and their pollutant outfall ceased. Magpie geese returned to that swamp. Today we associate the magpie goose with Arnhem Land in the tropical north, but in the contact period magpie geese and Cape Barren geese were common in Victoria. Massive swamp drainage and unsustainable shooting eliminated the birds from the state in just a few decades. One little accident of economic history was enough to revive the Warrnambool swamp and the birds returned. Imagine what we could do if we planned our environmental rejuvenation and refrained from exploiting those wonderful geese to the point of extinction.

Thirty years ago I worked with Ganai dancer and performer Jamie Thomas on a project to recover the magpie goose dance. Jamie had seen the return of the geese in that Warrnambool swamp and committed himself to the cultural revival of the dance. He found an old drawing of dancers bearing the goose design and we painted the chests of local men so that the dance could come back to life. It was an incredibly moving performance as that design had not been seen for a couple of centuries. The return of the geese was mirrored by the return of the people's association with them. It is not just a neat metaphor but a vital and strategic method of environmental and cultural recovery.

WARRIGAL GREENS AND CUNJIM WINYU

Warrigal greens or Captain Cook's spinach is a very common plant in Australia and New Zealand. James Cook found it growing as a bower over Aboriginal houses and stripped it to feed his sailors and successfully cure them of scurvy.[8]

That action says a lot. Numerous people, including historians and journalists, have argued with me that Governor Arthur Phillip and

Captain Cook were products of the Enlightenment, the period of anti-slavery and other human rights advances. Those were important moments for social justice, but how deeply did that enlightenment impact the colonial heart?

Taking the homegrown vegetables was a blunt message to the occupants of the houses. *You are nothing. We of the Enlightenment are here to take everything from you. We might write heartfelt messages of equality and fraternity but those rights do not extend to you. You are savages, and because of our religious superiority and the papal bull of 1493*[9] *we can take everything you have, including your life, land … and homegrown vegies.*

Warrigal greens are versatile and wonderfully nutritious plants. It has oxalic acid in the leaves but often at comparable levels to spinach.[10] Steaming or merely wilting them can dramatically lower the levels of oxalic acid but, in any case, they have high levels of vitamins and minerals and the plant is salt tolerant, which means it will grow in places where many other green vegetables cannot. It can be used in all the same applications as spinach and as the leaves stand up well to heat it is perfect in a stir-fry. Juvenile leaves can be eaten raw.

The bowering nature of warrigal greens makes it a very attractive plant but also allows it to provide great soil protection. In the summer of 2021 blue wrens and thornbills nested in our bower of greens.

When I was a kid we knew so little about Australian history that we had no idea that our old people grew vegetables. The tea-tree glades of Mornington in Victoria were festooned in climbing and bowering warrigal greens. We begged large packing boxes from the grocer and used them as toboggans to skid down the old sand dune slopes that were covered in the greens. The leaves are mucilaginous and provided excellent lubrication to the boxes. Our injuries amounted to not much more than we routinely applied to each other playing football. There were Aboriginal kids in that rough gang of boys but none of us knew that we were destroying a garden of spinach.

This is a vegetable that can grow almost anywhere, but its ability to grow in salty conditions (for example, the old coastal dunes of Mornington) and to tolerate soils of low nutrition, those old dune soils, make it a strong candidate to be an Australian staple. The plant requires no extra fertiliser, no extra water and no pesticides, all qualities that add dividends to the home and farm budget.

Cunjim winyu is a delightful salad vegetable. It has a small yellow button flower in summer, but during autumn and spring it has a lovely fresh green coronet and looks wonderful on top of a salad or in an open sandwich. We are selling this plant to local restaurants and I feel it is destined to be as much a mainstay of the Australian salad as tomatoes and basil. It grows on the margins of our salt swamp and is perennial so we don't have to till the soil or fertilise it and, like the greens, it tolerates salt, thus becoming a very important plant for a drying continent.

We served this vegetable to Ben Shewry, one of Australia's top chefs, in May 2021, and his eyes widened and he couldn't stop talking about it. This delight is in front of all Australians. The iceberg lettuce used to be the staple of Australian salads but here is our very own salad vegetable and overseas visitors will travel to Australia to taste the plant and see where it grows. Tourism Australia, here is your chance to satisfy the regularly stated demand of overseas tourists for Aboriginal language and cultural experience.

It has always astounded me that tourism entrepreneurs have failed to provide for this demand. Here is the opportunity but, as always, this is an Aboriginal plant and Aboriginal people must be part of the industry.

GRASSES

The colonial ethic meant that in order to justify invasion of a sovereign state's land, the rights of the original people of that land had to be repudiated. In Australia's case it began with attempts to say that Aboriginal and Torres Strait Islander people were barely human and that belief morphed into attempts to prove they did nothing with the land or were not even present.

Terra nullius is being more rigorously investigated, but its premise is still alive in the public consciousness after two and a half centuries in school curricula and political thought. In my home town I have often been told that no Aboriginal people lived there so there were no massacres and therefore no dispossession. These are not bad people. I went to their funerals because I loved them, and they remain a big part of my life, but it is very sad that good people can be so easily deluded.

Russell Mullet from the Ganai people of Bairnsdale found a map of Mallacoota being used as a drawer liner in the Department of Lands twenty years ago and passed it on to me. It was drawn by the surveyor Francis MacCabe in 1847, which is quite early in the

European history of the town. Shipwrecked sailors had walked through the area and Aboriginal Protector George Augustus Robinson visited in 1844,[11] but MacCabe's map shows every river, hill, promontory, island and plain named in the local Aboriginal language. As he did not speak the language, he must have received this information from Aboriginal informants. There is no more telling verification of Aboriginal occupancy than to scan the features of this map (see detail on pp. 48–51).

A volunteer at Yumburra discovered that there was a digital copy of the original MacCabe survey and we were stunned to find that, in its original form, it was coloured. When we offered the map for sale in 2018 there were few takers, but we have hopes that it will form a centrepiece of Mallacoota's history. We are donating a framed copy to the East Gippsland Shire to be displayed in the information centre so that residents and visitors can make up their own minds about the past. We also hope to display a copy at the Bushfire Recovery Hub at Mallacoota in an attempt to dispel the myth that there was no Aboriginal population in the area.

While today the whole district is dominated by forest, detailed descriptions on the document reveal vegetation zones across very open country, and areas of vegetation specialisation. Many of the flat areas are referred to as being dominated by 'herbage', while some are designated as grasslands, which means that Aboriginal people were managing some zones for herbage and others for grasses. The herbage was probably a combination of yam daisies, bulbine lilies, arthropodium, and others. These are all tubers, and within the forests today we can still find examples of them. These have been rare and remarkable finds but after the fires of 2020 opened up the canopy these plants made a resurgence.

One of the grasslands preserved in the district is at the Mallacoota Airport. The absence of stock or fertiliser has kept this land in conditions similar to those of the contact period. The dominant grass species is kangaroo grass and there are abundant orchids and other forbs. The area is slashed regularly as part of airport maintenance and, while the control burning of the local Bidwell and Yuin people has ceased, it is still dominated by grasses. Local cattlemen remember that this type of grassland once stretched all the way to Seal Creek in the west and that similar grasslands occurred on all coastal flats. These are the old Aboriginal agricultural zones. Thanks to the East Gippsland Shire, we have been allowed to harvest these grasses for seed and flour production since 2017. This experience has allowed us to reap our own grains, including microlaena, at Yumburra and to experiment with other grasses and sedges. While the yield per hectare might seem low, consider the advantages of not having to plough, irrigate, spray weeds or add fertiliser to the crops.

The extra advantage of being able to harvest these grasses within the forest itself offers new opportunities to manage our landscape for food and environmental protection. The canopy will have to be more open than it is today, but we will be able to cultivate grain on vast acreages, which will make the forest less vulnerable to wildfire. Cool burns between the trees in autumn will maintain this character.

The grasslands reported by early 'pioneers' and burnt by them to regenerate fresh growth became choked by banksia and casuarina once Australia became risk averse to any use of fire. National park

oumba

duga

Gheramburburraugh

gravelly land very little good grass and going west we find fresh water scarce

arrang elah

Turramundidg

Carragaragha honeysuckle and gum a

ences of open forest of apple stringybark

Bullungawah

quantity of good grass but fresh water is a long way back from the forest stringy bark and gum for the most part poor soil

G E N

Billymundalamah Toolgon

and not very abundant

Brolowe

Bianoughraugh R.

Gently sloping eminences thinly

Boidpoon

good herbage fresh water

gum

and

apple

Narroon

Weerywalloo

stringy bark

Walloon

Weliskah

Boej

Udammagauh

Talbaugh

E R

oll over forest of Stringybark

passed over forest country of stringybark up the inney saddle and took creek water... creek water very scarce

management is now endangering the survival of the rare ground parrot and eastern bristlebird because unchecked undergrowth is compromising the birds' prime habitat. This is not a deliberate but accidental hazard. Most rangers love country but we just need more sophisticated tools of management.

Conservationists are assessing the need for control burns to open up the country so that the birds' habitat can be recovered, but Australia's reluctance to follow Aboriginal cool-burning practice is inhibiting policy development. The dense scrubs that have developed in the 174 years since surveyor MacCabe first saw the district make any burning hazardous. It will have to be undertaken in careful mosaics and using the Aboriginal formula that Bidwell-Maap people gave to the Wangarabel resident Robert Alexander.[12] This formula was to begin cool burns after there had been three consecutive days of dew at the beginning of autumn and the wind had turned to the west.

It is salutary to note that Alexander had conducted massacres of Aboriginal people in the valley and yet the people still imparted this knowledge to him, such was their anxiety that the country should be cared for correctly.

Cool burning is a time-consuming method. Only small sections can be burnt at a time because the evening dews douse the progress of the fire. Aboriginal people waited for the season when those dews would be their friend. Today our forest managers avoid systems like this because they are slow and require a team of people to manage the fire. Our modern economy is averse to paying people to manage forest, but surely the fires of 2019–20 on the eastern seaboard tell us that there may be real savings in adopting methods that avoid destructive wildfires.

TUBERS

Murnong is an incredible vegetable resource that grew perennially without extra water, with no extra fertiliser other than ash from the horticultural burn every few years, and with no pesticide or weedicide. Edward Curr, an early 'settler' of land south of Echuca, recalled in 1841 that when he first entered that country 'the wheels of our dray used to turn them up [murnong] by the bushel'.[13] Today chefs extol its culinary qualities. The tuber and its leaves can be eaten raw as salad, and when the root is cooked in a slow pan the juices glisten like those of candied carrots. This is a new horticultural industry waiting to happen.

The white orchid that dominated the Melbourne plains was cultivated by Aboriginal people as a major food source, as were cinnamon bells or potato orchids.[14] These plants have large nutritious tubers and were so well managed that they grew in abundance. Now, the white orchid is almost extinct because of habitat loss, soil compaction and the depredations of sheep.[15] How can we as horticulturalists and agriculturalists tolerate the loss of such a valuable food plant? It makes no economic sense. If our tolerance of such loss is to rationalise the invasion and what it has meant for the ecology and economy of the colony, then it is a very heavy price to pay for peace of mind. At Yumburra it is our ambition to grow the white orchid in tubestock for distribution to Aboriginal food groups in the Melbourne district.

The tubers we are currently harvesting became rare in the district once sheep and cattle were introduced. Not all farmers will isolate their flocks of sheep and herds of cattle from tuber crops, but those who do will never have to plough their land again. The tuber crops can grow in tandem with grasses, and because all are perennial with large root systems, they improve the soil. This is such a dramatic change in agricultural method that many will be wisely sceptical until its advantages are proven. Not all farmlands have to be managed like this for Australia to reap the benefits of safer forests.

Initially the marginal lands where farm profits are low or debts have driven farmers away will be suitable for trials, but if our experience at Yumburra is any guide, the advantages will soon speak for themselves. By avoiding the need to plough, we also allow the mycorrhizal fungi to build symbiotic relationships with the roots of other plants in a manner that enhances the productivity of both. This is a botanical and chemical interaction that is destroyed by ploughing and applications of chemical fertilisers.[16]

We are trialling harvest methods for several tubers because we have to rediscover the old Aboriginal management techniques. We know from colonial records that Aboriginal growers were able to lift the plant to harvest some of the tubers while leaving the rest undisturbed. Once selected tubers were harvested, the plant was pressed back into the ground to regrow. We have had some success with this method but need to do more work so that we cause less disturbance to the plant. We also need to find the best harvest sequence.

This year our trials for tubers will begin outside our enclosed gardens. Weeding is one of the things we need to refine. Aboriginal people removed seedling wattles and eucalypts from tuber and grass crops. We will need to cool burn beneath the trees to inhibit scrub when we try to replicate the old system of growing these crops under the canopy of a more open forest. How much weeding and burning will be required to maintain the balance between food plants and forest plants? The fires of 2019–20 showed us the merit of a forest comprising fewer but larger trees, but the methods required to attain that balance are part of our research effort on the farm.

We are committing ourselves to a program that we know will take seventy years to complete. It has taken 230 years for our forests to reach their current stage of flammability, so seventy years is a modest period in which to expect a correction to occur. But first and foremost we must stop hating big trees.

APPLES, CHERRIES, CURRANTS AND RASPBERRIES

Kangaroo apple (*Solanum laciniatum*) is a very beautiful and quick-growing tree. It likes disturbed or burnt ground and so provides great protection for traumatised soils. The very sweet fruit must be eaten ripe but the birds know this too, so unprotected plants are raided early each day by honeyeaters, bowerbirds, wattlebirds and currawongs.

Aboriginal people picked it before it was completely ripe and stored it in sand.[17] This may have been to aid ripening or merely to protect it from animals. The fruit also lends itself to preservation. Perhaps it was treated like bush tomatoes and quandong, which were packed into wads in the manner of fig paste and so could be used as travelling food or as a condiment or flavouring.[18]

At Yumburra we are raising kangaroo apple from seed and the prospects for its use are very good. But, sorry to harp on this, how are

Aboriginal people to be included in its use? That is the question we must keep asking, not to be good and kind Christians but because there is a moral obligation placed on us to acknowledge sovereign intellectual property.

We have always eaten the little cherries off cherry ballart (*Exocarpos cupressiformis*) trees. These trees are a magnificent dark green and form associations with the trees around them. The wood is good for boomerangs and implements, and owls like to roost in the branches because the dense foliage provides terrific cover. The fruit is small and slightly musky but is high in vitamins B and C. At Yumburra we are experimenting with drop sheets to collect the fruit: a good shake of the tree allows ripe fruit to collect on the sheet beneath. There may not be a commercial way to harvest it, but we will keep trying and at any rate it is a beautiful tree and the fruit is a bonus. The trees should be protected in their own right because they are very slow growing and an important part of the ecosystem here: many animals and insects depend on them. They also seem to be quite fire resistant. Most survived the fire at Yumburra and provided solace when other trees were burnt black.

The native currant (*Coprosma quadrifida*) is a delicious fruit. It is tiny but full of flavour and vitamins. We have been harvesting it by tapping the trunk and branches so that the ripe fruit falls into a coolamon or onto a drop sheet. This is a time-consuming task and may make the fruit's commercial use problematic, but for the home gardener it is a boon. No diseases, no water demand, no need to use fertiliser and a really attractive plant. The fruits make a zesty addition to salads and ice cream but eaten straight off the tree they are superb.

The plant that I think has most commercial potential is the native raspberry (*Rubus parvifolius*). This was my Uncle Bill's favourite fruit and he would get us to hunt the gullies to keep him supplied. It is not as juicy as a commercial strawberry or raspberry but it is highly nutritious and, typical of Australian plants, flourishes in Australian conditions. It is a vigorous ground cover but also likes to climb over other plants and shrubs. It does not have to be coddled like its European namesake and forms a natural part of the garden. I used to think the yield from this rambling plant was small, but one year at Yumburra it grew within the protection of an enclosed garden and its bounty was prolific. With possums, birds, bush rats and goannas excluded it became an important fruit for us. We are now encouraging Aboriginal communities to grow it in gardens and vineyards.

KURRAJONG

One of the local Aboriginal people working at Yumburra, Chris Harris, took us on an exploration of country up at Yambulla, an old property in the Australian Alps, where the owner was keen for us to harvest his kangaroo and spear grasses. Chris was interested in the kurrajong (*Brachychiton populneus*) on the property as he had learnt from his father and grandfather that his people used to eat the root of the young tree. Yuin people used the slender rods of the coppicing kurrajong to make spears and fire drills, and continue that practice today. The fruit was also eaten after the sharp bristles were removed.

Chris had been taught about the palatability of the young tree's root. He dug up a small tree, and we found that the root was sweet and filling. We are experimenting now with growing seedling kurrajong trees to see if we can harvest the roots for food, and have planted them as an avenue in the driveway of Yumburra in a style that the old people used prior to invasion. The current owner of a property at Pambula found an avenue that had been deliberately set out in corridor formation to direct attention to a local mountain, and we have followed that example to lead people to the heart of our farm. This is the sort of thing we try to do consistently in our working day in order to honour our old people.

GRAINS AND BREAD

Why are budgerigars disappearing? Early European 'explorers' and 'settlers' commented that the centre of Australia was often seemingly carpeted with these birds, but today the seeds on which they once flourished have been destroyed by cattle, sheep, goats, donkeys, horses and buffalo, all voracious hard-hoofed animals that compact the soil and reduce its fertility and moisture retention. The loss of these plants and the habitat and ground cover they provided is a serious national disgrace. Aboriginal clans grieve for their old plants and their foods and medicines.

The areas where Mitchell reported grasses higher than his horses' saddles and where Charles Sturt was saved by people feeding him bread baked from the grass seeds they had harvested in what is now known as Sturt Stony Desert[19] are today virtually devoid of grass. Attempts to grow rice and cotton, plants from other climate zones, have caused the soil to blow across Sydney. The media treat this annual event as one more example of the continent being hostile towards us instead of us being hostile to the continent. Anyway, we have our own rices, which will soon be in high demand if we make wise economic decisions. They grow in various parts of Australia, some in pure sand.[20] Asia is very interested in these products; it is only Australia that seems uninterested.

Sorghum is another plant that is surely going to be useful to us. Australian sorghum varieties have been depleted by land clearance and feral herbivores but are still present in isolated pockets of our landscape. They have large seeds and grow abundantly, and were used for flour making by the old people. Where is the agricultural science community? We need to investigate this plant but, red flag! red flag!, we must include Aboriginal people in its bounty.

When Burke and Wills were dying on Cooper Creek the local Aboriginal people offered them nardoo flour made from seeds harvested from *Marsilea drummondii*, a plant that grew in the ephemeral lakes. The local people soaked the seeds overnight to leach a toxin, but Burke and Wills ignored this process and suffered because of it. More culinary help might have been forthcoming, an assistance most British chefs required, but as Burke chose to shoot his pistol at the people, communications became abbreviated.[21] The habit of nardoo to flourish in shallow lakes and produce seed when a lake dries out makes harvesting easy. On a drying continent, a plant that produces flour under such difficult conditions might need to be investigated.

While writing *Dark Emu* I was intimidated by the learning curve I had to ascend. How could I have been so ignorant? Bread was one of those provocations to real learning. Aboriginal-baked products had been labelled as crude dampers. (The word 'damper' is probably taken from an Aboriginal language: *dangar* is an east-coast word for bread products, and it is probable that Europeans pinched it.) I assumed that our bread was inferior to the European staple because this is what my sixteen years of education had taught me to expect. The reality shamed me. I buried myself in library after library and eventually the Melbourne Museum as I researched the world's first breads. Grinding stones in Kakadu have been examined recently and show that flour production was well established there 65,000 years ago.[22] This is long before any other society was known to make bread. So Aboriginal Australians were the world's first bakers.

I set myself on a journey of discovery. Were there any examples of contact-period bread still available for study? I was told of an ancient bread that had been stolen from an Aboriginal oven and was housed in the Yarrabah museum in Far North Queensland. Judy Watson, the Murri artist, had seen it a few years before and rang to let me know of its existence. I wanted to examine the bread to find its ingredients, cooking method and rising agent, but when the Abbott government slashed Aboriginal funding in 2014, the museum had to close and the dispersal of the collection caused the bread to be lost.

Thankfully, Aboriginal people were determined to explore the probability that more examples existed. Museum collection records had no mention of Aboriginal 'bread'. I am not exaggerating the impact of ignorance on the assumptions of Australian research, partly because knowledge of Australian Aboriginal life is so minimal that it was assumed Aboriginal people did not cook. And if they did, who cared? Science in this area has therefore been hampered.

For hundreds of years very few researchers bothered with such collections because 'real' research of this type was concentrated in Egypt and the Fertile Crescent, where 'real' civilisation began. Many Australians of European heritage have long thought that any civilisation could only come from the region where their culture developed. This impediment is one of the reasons Australians have taken so long to recognise Aboriginal achievement. Today there is much more interest, and researchers are exploring museum holdings and conducting intensive archaeological investigations. The stories of our country told to our grandchildren will be far more subtle and comprehensive than the mandatory two pages of misinformation delivered in my education.

Anyway, a team at Melbourne Museum that included Aboriginal and non-Aboriginal curators set out to research their collection. The word 'bread' was a distraction because early collectors had refused to use it when referring to Aboriginal baking. That word, like 'house', had to be reserved for Europeans. Such collection objects, I discovered, are catalogued as 'seed cakes' or 'food samples'. Finally, I got a call to say they had found a catalogue entry of an item that was found in an Aboriginal oven, but when we examined that drawer we found it empty. Objects, I am later told, are often moved for conservation treatment, research and community access.

Then there was a breakthrough in my quest. I was called in to examine fifteen loaves that had been discovered by entering different

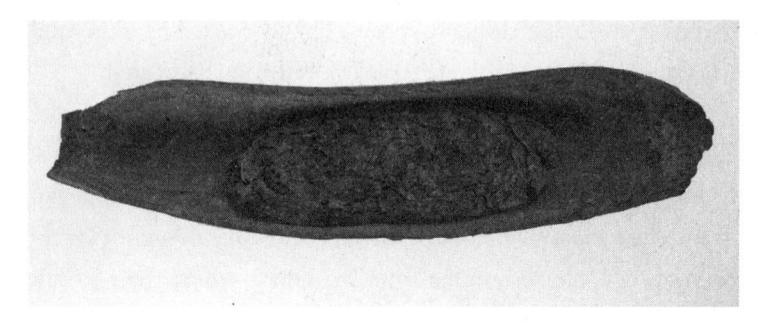

Bread in coolamon. Kaytetye people, Barrow Creek, Northern Territory, 1901.

Bark container (top), grinding stone (left) and bread (right). Ngukurr (Roper River), Eastern Arnhem Land, Northern Territory, 1911.

Nardoo seeds (detail)

Bread. Wambaya people, McArthur River, Northern Territory, 1901.

search terms in the database. Museum staff had collated all the records of food samples (and other possible variations of relevant search terms) for my research of breads and foods. I arrived with real trepidation, having been disappointed so many times, but there they were, breads. They were so beautiful, so important, that I cried. I was so proud of my people's chemistry. The breads were risen and some were fitted into the curve of the coolamon they had been placed in. I was in awe of the beauty of this domestic ritual, the genius of Aboriginal life, and acutely aware of what this could mean for Australia's agricultural sustainability.

Back to the bread. What was the rising agent? A group of young Aboriginal women whose homelands are spread across Australia asked me to visit them at the Art Gallery of New South Wales, where they were involved in cooking workshops. I asked them about the rising agents for our bread and challenged them to ask their elders. Over the next few months I got half-a-dozen responses. One student was told about the method of steeping banksia flowers in water and allowing them to ferment; one had a grandfather who had been a camp cook and had added the whitest ash from a particular wood to bread. Another said her grandfather used to shoot galahs and use the partly fermented seed from the birds' crop as a rising agent – and then he cooked the galah.

(One of many Australian myths is about the difficulty of cooking galah: throw a stone in the pot with the galah and when the rock is tender the galah is cooked. Galahs can live to be over 100 years old, so I suppose if you can't tell the difference between a geriatric galah and a young bird you deserve to eat rock.)

The existence of the Melbourne Museum breads is of huge importance to Australia. To be able to make bread from perennial grain fields has enormous significance for the second-driest continent on earth. Aboriginal people worked with the actual environmental conditions of this continent rather than expect her to grow the grains of a different hemisphere. The breads represent a way for us to reconsider how we use Mother Earth.

ABORIGINAL BEE FARMING

As an indication of how far we are from fully appreciating the extent of Aboriginal agriculture, a paper contributed to *The Australasian Beekeeper* analyses the method used by Aboriginal people to farm native bees.[23] The investigation describes a fascinating process of Indigenous hiving.

Being able to farm and utilise the honey from Australian bees would be a very useful way of future-proofing the Australian honey industry, given the dangers posed by European foulbrood disease.

Simply being open to Aboriginal expertise may create a new industry for Australia and, as mentioned so many times in this book, provide an entrepreneurial and employment opportunity for Aboriginal people.

I have shared some very important Aboriginal knowledge in this chapter and I am nervous about that, given Australia's propensity for theft. But I challenge you to ensure that any use you make of that knowledge, or even the intellectual comfort of its acceptance, comes with your insistence that Aboriginal people are included in this new industry. Think of it like a return on invested capital; black capital.

4

FUTURE FARMING

Like plant exploitation, protein exploitation must be looked at differently by Australians. The world is at war over protein: a few have more than they need and most have too little. In the colonial period many European witnesses referred to the light tilth of Australian soils, but some also commented on the deterioration as soon as sheep and cattle were introduced. The hard-hoofed animals denuded the vegetation and compacted the soils, causing erosion and plummeting soil fertility. Today when we see flourishing farms they are either supported by chemical additives at great expense and loss of soil health, or are still spending the accumulated black capital of careful land management.

The invaders were desperate to turn the country into a little England, and in doing so imported animals that have since done untold damage to the landscape. Is it too late to wish that the country had been more loved for itself by those so desperate to steal it? Why introduce a rabbit when you already had bandicoots? Why introduce a fox when there were no 'gentlemen' to hunt it?

KANGAROOS AND EMUS

Every farm grazes kangaroos or emus, sometimes both. They are largely pest free, especially when the animals graze on land not populated by sheep or cattle, and the meat is much leaner than that of most other grazing stock. It ought to be part of an economically clever country's diet, and yet we have never farmed these animals.

Why do we ignore this obvious source of protein? Australian animals do not need coddling behind fences or require hard feeding in winter. Is the reluctance to eat them because they are on our coat of arms which, I am told, first appeared in *Australasian Post* as a cartoon in between the pin-up girls and racist jokes? Or do we slavishly cling to farming European animals because we know how to manage their herds and flocks? It makes no sense, in my opinion, to ignore their protein just because kangaroos bounce or, in the case of emus, flounce.

One of the great joys of country life is to see relaxed and contented animals. Kangaroos around a farm will seek out shade on a hot day and mothers will spoon up with their joeys and often rest a forepaw on the young's shoulder. It really touches my heart to find them so relaxed within vicinity of our house. But a calf or a lamb is pretty cute too, and yet we send them off over thousands of kilometres to be slaughtered in dreadful conditions. If we are to eat meat, then we have to take responsibility for the butchering.

Grazing cattle and sheep requires that we drench them and treat them for footrot, lice, worms, bloat, scours, pinkeye, mastitis, flystrike, pneumonia and a hundred more health problems. Most grazing animals are chemically treated, and for most chemicals there is a period following the application that the meat cannot be eaten.[1] Kangaroos and emus, adapted to Australian conditions, need no such treatment when not grazing on land heavily populated by domestic stock and therefore per pound of flesh they are very economical.

To harvest these animals, Aboriginal people used droving techniques of such steady progress that the creatures were not frightened into panicked flight. They were slowly guided between the wide wings of battues. The animals were moved gradually so that they didn't panic ... and bounce. The wings of the battues might be 40 kilometres apart in the beginning, which meant that the droving was a community activity conducted over a few days.[2] The design of some battues can still be seen[3] and suggests that the wings funnelled the animals towards small holding yards where beasts were selected for slaughter, most often young males. Much more research needs to go into studying this style of droving and the remnants of their construction. Aboriginal people also corralled young pelicans,[4] and other species were herded, so the slow droving of kangaroos is hardly surprising. The old people used spears and net traps for emus and other birds, but communities also combined to drove them slowly to designated areas. The battue funnel seems like a possibility for modern application. It would require much less fencing than our current square paddocks demand. A system of shares would need to be organised to reward all the different landholders, but is it much different from fishing?

There is another avenue of protein collection we might consider. Every morning in East Gippsland the road toll becomes apparent, with carcasses of wallabies, kangaroos, possums and wombats every kilometre or so. In this district it is not uncommon to find kangaroos and wallabies with broken legs as the result of being hit by a car. I will never forget finding one huge injured male by following his moans of agony. And I will certainly never forget the look he turned on me when I arrived with my gun. He knew exactly what was about to happen, and was ready.

We harvest these animals with our cars, so why not use their bounty instead of allowing their carcasses to bloat? If we are going to be meat eaters, and there are good arguments for some meat in our diet, then let us be economical about our harvest. We often check the pouches of these dead or wounded animals for young that might be revived in shelters, but we also butcher some carcasses and routinely harvest the tail tendons for the purpose of making traditional artefacts.

Animals killed like this almost always die suddenly, without the meat-toughening release of adrenaline into their system. Why don't we have patrol vans with people licensed to inspect roadkill and harvest anything left that is fit for human consumption or could be made into dog food? A simple temperature probe is almost all that is required. Older carcasses could be moved further off the highway so that eagles and crows were not tempted to feed too close to the road. Stringent health and refrigeration rules could be set in place so that we don't waste any resources. Harvesting that meat and the kangaroo and emu stock in our paddocks would mean we could afford to graze fewer hard-hoofed animals.

SEAFOOD

A similar conservative approach could be used in our oceans and rivers. Today's fishing methods are often incredibly crude. For example, seagrasses are vital for the survival of hundreds of creatures and yet scallop fishing ploughs right through them. This practice destroys the seagrasses and kills millions of worms and crustacea in the process. Fish stocks plummet as a result of the crudity of this operation.[5]

Apollo Bay, in south-western Victoria, used to be home to massive schools of barracouta. The schools were plundered and shovelled onto trucks which then undertook the slow crawl up the Otway Ranges and on to the fish market in Footscray. Often, by the time they arrived, as much as 100 per cent of the catch had begun to spoil and was no longer suitable for human consumption.[6] But that did not stop the fishers. 'See fish, must have fish' was the mantra. Of course the fishery collapsed when the schools were harvested beyond their capability to maintain numbers.

Crayfish, or southern rock lobster, are now in the same precarious position. The industry is trying to prove its sustainability, but the damage might already be too great.[7] One local bay used to be red with the creatures, according to locals, but those days are over. My father used to buy a crayfish every Friday night for a few bob but today they are A$120 a kilo.

Chinese and Japanese demand hoicks the price of crayfish, making them very expensive for Australians, but it is overfishing that is the greatest danger to our enjoying seafood into the future. I used to get a crayfish for old Uncle Banjo Clarke every now and then, and he was always quick to inspect it to see what sex it was. The day I gave him a female resulted in the most gentle lecture on sustainability I have ever received. He was a beautiful man but a stern conservationist. Never kill females unless you want populations to decrease.

Bycatch, the incidental capture and destruction of untargeted fish and seabirds in fishing nets, is something we should not tolerate. Some nets have been improved so that bycatch is reduced, but it is still unsustainable, as evidenced by New South Wales losing 30 per cent of its reef fish stocks in the past ten years. If that is repeated in the next decade, our fish stocks may be on an ever-downward spiral.

We must demand that we don't catch unwanted fish in the pursuit of the small number of desirable species. The industry must participate in this science but before beginning must agree that our current methods are part of the problem. Targeted fishing methods must be scrupulous in their conservancy and young fisherpeople must be inculcated with the community expectation that their industry will provide a sustainable fishery for their grandchildren.

Our resource use has been exacerbated by an exploding world population and excessive food consumption by the developed world. Restraint in both population growth and individuals' eating habits will go a long way to conserving our oceans. The industry will find this hard to accept but surely they were never promised to be the last fishing generation on earth. Everybody must plan for a future fishery and there will have to be changes. Fisherpeople will feel the pinch of reduced demand and consumers will have to wear the higher prices, but we all know that the alarm is ringing for fish stocks around the globe. Doing nothing is just petulance and selfishness.

We need to look at our country through Australian rather than European eyes. There is a limit to how much you can force a geography to bend to your will, and we should stay well inside that limit on account of the commercial wisdom of not killing the golden goose. The country is telling us that we are throttling her. The massive incidence of erosion after 1800[8] should have been a warning, as should the emergence of wildfire around the same time.[9] Mallee soil ending up in Melbourne and Port Phillip Bay was a cry for help. Salination in the irrigation districts was another omen. The destruction of the Murray-Darling Basin was a huge red flag, but our response to that flag was to privatise the common wealth water.

We need to swallow our pride and examine the principles of the first farmers, who were responding to the continent as they found it. Change was implemented in the way fire was used and water deployed, but it was within the limits of continental tolerance. The science was radically different to our own, but societies evolve all the time and it is our actions in that change that count. We can be Christian and reward capital but still avoid massive fish kills, erosion and species extinction. The Western world believes our science defines us, so let's rationalise that science for the Southern

Hemisphere and rationalise capitalism to fit the needs of the planet. Is it rational to allow some to have gold-plated taps and for others to have no water? If globalism worked, this wouldn't need stating. Selfishness and pride should not be seen as the keystones of our system. We go on about freedoms and liberty, but too few have too much of those things and bear no responsibility. We should tax their liberty so that they do not destroy our home. This is not class envy, it is rational economic science. I don't care if some receive the world's water through a golden tap as long as everybody has a tap.

The current methods of fishing are efficient if the only consideration is price on the plate, but if we add in the health of the ocean they are impossibly unsustainable. We need to pay the real price of forest products, and therefore become more conservative in their use, and the same goes for fish. The cost to the environment must be factored into the price on the plate. It will be disgraceful if our flagrant habits mean we are the last generation to enjoy eating fish. Everything we do has to be geared towards tomorrow. We must imagine our great-grandchildren and pledge ourselves to leaving them with a beautiful world, not one depleted by our waste and greed.

5

COUNTRY

[T]here was another instrument in the hands of these savages which must be credited with results which it would be difficult to over-estimate. I refer to the *fire-stick*; for the blackfellow was constantly setting fire to the grass and trees ... he tilled his land and cultivated his pastures with fire ... it may perhaps be doubted whether any section of the human race has exercised a greater influence on the physical condition of any large portion of the globe than the wandering savages of Australia.[1]

In 1883 the Victorian squatter Edward Curr eloquently captured how closely the people of 1788 worked with fire, but missed a significant truth. Doing nothing also causes change. 'No fire' is an active category. It is not merely the absence of fire. It has ecological impact, Law and ceremony. It dominated high-rainfall areas but even in desert it mattered. Fire shapes our continent, and no fire – deliberately not burning – is part of its story.

What was Australia like in 1788? Much we would recognise, for much is found nowhere else. But a visit back to 1788 would be full of surprises, commonest where newcomers have crowded most densely, but visible everywhere. Australia has always surprised newcomers. Those who came soon after 1788 were almost permanently surprised by the wonders they saw. Today the biggest surprise would be how much the land has changed since 1788. Many of us assume that how the land looks now was pretty well always so, but new people, plants, animals, pests, diseases and technology have come, native plants and creatures have gone, and the face of the land has changed dramatically. Australia is a world leader in species extinction, species reduction and land degradation.

Early newcomers saw abundance: well-spaced mobs of grazing animals, skies flocked with birds, waters black with fish. Long after 1788 the clear waters of both Sydney Harbour and many inland rivers let people see the bottom, and great shoals of fish 'floating like birds in mid-air', as Thomas Mitchell put it on the Darling.[2] In the Kimberley men wrote of country abounding 'in every description of game' – fish, birds, animals and reptiles[3] – and in 1921 an upper Darling and Paroo pioneer recalled with admiration

> the condition of the country, the growth of the trees and bushes, such as sheoaks, pines, and acacias and a score of other kinds of trees

> that bushfires always destroy were, when the white man arrived, flourishing in the perfection of beauty and health ... Encounter Bay [SA] and the neighbourhood was a striking example of the care exercised by the original inhabitants to preserve the plant life, and incidentally animal life. The country was clothed with beauty to the very margin of the sea. The numerous ti-tree swamps were a very aviary of bird life. Much of all this is gone now by the white man's destroying hand in the march of civilisation ... I think it may be stated to the credit of the Australian savage that such [management] was the case over most of the continent when the white man assumed possession.[4]

Newcomers wrought carnage on such abundance. At least seventy species have gone extinct since 1788 – most estimates think more. At least 120 are critically endangered. This reflects a staggering level of ignorance and incompetence.

Inland birds like galahs, crested pigeons and little corellas have spread,[5] but especially on offshore islands other birds have become extinct, while ground dwellers from emus and cassowaries to mallee fowl, curlews and quail, and birds like eagles, black swans, wrens and some cockatoos and parrots have shrunk their range, some into refuges. In the terrible Gippsland fires of 6 February 1851, two children were saved from the flames by hiding under the bodies of birds that dropped from the sky.[6] Nowhere are there enough birds even to imagine that now.

Reptiles have declined: over twenty species are critically endangered. As well as habitat loss, newcomers wage war on snakes, and settlement and random fire have reduced some lizards, skinks and frogs to pockets. Two insect species, plus almost certainly others we don't know of, have gone extinct, and insects in general are fewer – including on car windscreens.

Animals have gone, many from arid areas where fire and no fire underlay their food cycle. Eastern grey kangaroos and possibly possums have increased, but thylacines and several smaller marsupials are extinct, while koalas (though not common in 1788), platypus, and smaller animals like dunnarts, bilbies, greater gliders, bandicoots, quolls and *mala* (rufous hare-wallaby) are in the queue for extinction. In the last 200 years a third of the world's mammals made extinct have been Australian.[7] Sometimes we didn't even notice their going until too late. In central deserts mala were once abundant and a staple, but shifting people off country let fuel build up, causing hot fires that destroyed plant cover and exposed mala to cats and foxes. In its home range it went extinct about 1991 but is now being reintroduced from breeding sanctuaries.

These are losses we can count. Changes to the land, slow, subtle, often irreversible, are harder to see, but literally basic.

Topsoil has compacted under vehicles and hoofed animals, or blown or washed away. Stream banks display exposed tree roots crouched claw-like over the water, and dryland carries roots rising stick-like up to 2 metres above the ground or fallen into deep erosion gullies. What once sheltered them has gone.

Subsoil has changed. Salt lies under much of Australia, but it has surfaced menacingly since 1788. Land not salt then is saline now.

Water cutting deeper lifts salt. Salt kills plants. Along south-east inland rivers, giant river red gums healthy sixty years ago are dead. Off water too, soil has salinated. Topsoil erosion, deep ploughing, clearing native perennial grasses can cause this. Even planting trees can cause it: since fresh water sits above salt water, trees that drink it let salt water rise. The more and bigger the trees the more fresh water they drink, and the more readily salt rises to kill them.

Water has gone. Even fast coastal streams generally ran slower in 1788. Native grasses slowed flows off feeder slopes, and streams choked with debris. Slow streams run shallow. Big rivers like the Murray and the Darling had frequent fords along them, while on the lower Murrumbidgee what were once *dis*tributary creeks are now tributaries: they have reversed flow, because since 1788 the river has cut below them.

Shallow streams flood readily. In hill country near Gundagai in 1834, George Bennett remarked on the Murrumbidgee's many 'swamps about its banks, overflown during floods, and even now [a dry time] absorbing a large quantity of water'.[8] Wide-spreading water was common. In a dry continent it would seem obvious to keep water in the landscape, yet newcomers cut channels and drain swamps enthusiastically, letting them imagine that today's dry stream margins were always there. In paddocks black soil or reeds marking former swamps lie near the farm dams that replaced them. Governments drain on a bigger scale, such as behind South Australia's Coorong, so more land is dry than in 1788, meaning fewer summer-saving wetlands and fewer refuges from drought and fire.

Today newcomers often respond to environmental degradation by planting trees, or promising to. National Tree Day assumes that tree cover has declined since 1788. In some places that's true, but overall there are probably more trees now, differently distributed. Fewer trees on farmland, endangering woodland habitats, are outbalanced by denser forests, trees capturing grass, rainforest advancing, parks and reserves filling in untended. It is common now to see dense swathes of young eucalypts growing straight up, often with hardly a grandmother tree in sight. They are dense because the seedlings were freed from fire, and they grow straight because in dense forest they must race for light. In the open those same eucalypts spread wide, and even on forest edges they push branches out to the light. Generations ago they weren't there at all – grass was. Look around: whipstick is probably our most common forest. A National Grass Day would make more sense.

Forest often grows a dense scrub understorey, a fire fuse, ready to lift flame into the canopy. Much, not all, forest was open in 1788. Horses and drays could pass unimpeded, and early travellers, notably in western Tasmania, wrote casually of walking distances in times and places Olympic marathoners could not match now. Today we are so used to a scrubby understorey that we think it was always there.

Grass, not trees, was central to healthy country in 1788. Grassland carried many useful plants, and most animals with most meat. It was a firebreak, it made seeing and travelling easier, and it confined forest, making forest resources more predictable. Almost always it took the best soil, and probably there was more grass then than now.

But less native grass. Spinifex has spread, cane grass and blady grass may be much the same, but native fodder perennials that once dominated, especially in the south – kangaroo, wallaby, spear, poa, millet – are sparser. Dormant in winter and ripening in late summer, their tan heads blanketed the land, shielding it from drought and providing feed in the season feed is now hardest to find. Today's introduced crops and weeds tend to be green in winter and dead white in late summer. The upset of our native perennials changed the colour of Australia. It is hard to say whether a traveller from 1788 would notice first this colour change, or the scrub understorey.

Herbs, tubers, lilies and orchids lived in the spaces Australia's tussock perennials provided, or in forest or swamp shelter. They flourish after fire: for example the first spring after the 1983 and 2003 fires saw a flush of flowers that newcomers had not thought possible. In later years they declined as shrub cover increased, much of their habitat smothered or let decay.

Why should the land have changed so much? Why should Australia, so recently invaded, generally so sparsely occupied, be so prominent in degradation and species extinction and reduction?

The people in charge have changed. Australia was not natural in 1788, but made. It was an artefact. It was not land, but Country. 'Country' is an English word Aboriginal people have transformed. Country is physical, communal and spiritual – land, water, sky, habitats, sites, places, totems and relationships, a world of the mind, a way of believing and behaving. Creator ancestors made Country in the Dreaming, and they still oversee it. Not only obvious features that newcomers name, but every pebble and ripple disclosed both the ecological logic of its existence and the Dreaming's presence. Here wallaby and wallaby ancestor live, there nardoo and nardoo ancestor, there avenging fire killed lawbreakers, here a punishing flood reached. Anthropologist Ted Strehlow well depicted

> the overwhelming affection felt by a native for his ancestral territory. Mountains and creeks and springs and water-holes are, to him, not merely interesting or beautiful ... [but] the handiwork of ancestors from whom he himself has descended. He sees recorded in the surrounding landscape the ancient story of the lives and the deeds of the immortal beings whom he reveres ... The whole countryside is his living, age-old family tree. The story of his own totemic ancestor is to the native the account of his own doings at the beginning of time, at the dim dawn of life, when the world as he knows it now was being shaped and moulded by all-powerful hands. He himself has played a part in that first glorious adventure ... Gurra said to me: 'The Ilbalintja soak has been defiled by the hands of the white men ... No longer do men pluck up the grass and the weeds and sweep the ground clean around it; no longer do they care for the resting place of Karora ... [but] It still holds me fast; and I shall tend it while I can; while I live, I shall love to gaze on this ancient soil.'[9]

In this way of seeing, nothing is wilderness, all must be cared for. The driest corner is as much Country as the richest park, a spiritual endowment far more important than any economic value newcomers might give it. Every place is filled with presences, rights and duties, binding people for life to keep Country alive. Some places might not be touched for years, but not for a moment do carers forget them. Far from home, people dream their Country and yearn to be part of it once more.

The Dreaming, a religious philosophy rooted in ecology, subjects all life to overwhelming religious sanction. In north-east Tasmania late in 1830 a small band of survivors led by Mannalargenna showed how powerful this sanction was. The Black Line, a military cordon bent on capturing every surviving Tasmanian, was under way, and white men were searching to deport the band offshore. The hunted people knew that smoke would betray them, yet still they fired the land, in the face of death toiling to do what perhaps ten times as many would once have done. Nothing shows so clearly how crucial land care was. It was a mortal duty, a levy on the souls of brave men and women.[10]

The Dreaming has two basic rules: obey the Law, and leave the world as you found it – not better or worse, for God judges that, but the same. There is change of course: seasons turn, kangaroos graze grass into lawns, ants stitch leaves, kites and brown hawks drop burning sticks to start a new fire, bettong digging softens soil letting plants take hold, all as their totems predict and expect. But changes are cyclic: each must and will return to the balance the creator ancestors made. As a Ramingining (NT) elder neatly put it, 'The seasons are not about the passing of time. They are about how things link together ... Everything is part of a rhythm.'[11]

The Dreaming compelled this via totems. Everything with shape – people, ancestors, animals, plants, stars, earth, wind, diseases, introduced species like rabbits, camels and house flies – has a totem derived from a creator ancestor, otherwise it can't exist. Every totem has people who belong to it, and at the risk of their souls must care for it. An emu man must care for emus and emu habitat, and they must care for him, and so on. This bond was illustrated in western Victoria in March 1854, when Assistant Protector of Aborigines William Thomas

> was out with a celebrated Western Port black tracking five other blacks. The tracks had been lost some days at a part of the country where we expected they must pass. We ran down a creek; after going some miles a bear [koala] made a noise as we passed. The black stopped, and a parley commenced. I stood gazing alternately at the black and the bear. At length my black came to me and said, 'Me big one stupid; bear tell me no go you that way.' We immediately crossed the creek, and took a different track. Strange as it may appear, we had not altered our course above one and a half miles before we came upon the tracks of the five blacks, and never lost them after.[12]

Man and 'bear' were the same totem, so as well as a general duty to all life, each had immutable obligations to the other, which each neglected at the risk of the very existence of their totem, including of course them.

Totems embraced habitats. To mention a koala place was and is to signal an ecological association of plants, animals and features: the eucalypts koalas like, the grasses, bushes, bulbs and tubers that grow best among those eucalypts, the animals, birds, reptiles and insects that favour that country, the fire and water that maintain it, the creator ancestors who made it, and the people who care for it. This immutable fusion of Law and ecology made the whole continent a single estate, expressed on the ground and in art and song and dance by Songlines.

Songlines are not totems, but they too are ecologically grounded, either explaining and maintaining a habitat or, as with the Seven Sisters and Native Cat Songlines, paying heed to ecology in their epic travels across the land. Every tiny part of land, sea and sky, every totem, is part of at least one Songline.

Ecologist Alan Newsome showed one Songline's ecological associations west of Alice Springs. He studied the major totem sites along a Red Kangaroo Songline and found that each coincided with 'the most favourable habitat' for the roos, notably where range washouts grew the best grass. Conversely, whenever the red kangaroo ancestor flies through the sky or goes underground, it avoids an unfavourable habitat. The Songline describes the land from a red kangaroo viewpoint, with a clear conservation imperative. It prescribes where red kangaroos have protected refuges, conservation reserves, Country. When in good seasons numbers build up and some move out beyond these safe limits, those can be hunted.[13]

Fire is a totem, and it can influence totems by allocating plants to totems according to their flammability. It appears in Songlines, sometimes is decisive in them, but unlike all Creation except people it is not particular to any of them. Instead it is an instrument of Law, as people are. Fire and people need and help each other. Without people there would be no fire; without fire there would be no people. Both need the rest of Creation, but together they envelop Country and Dreaming alike, in a perpetual alliance on which all the rest depends.

6

AN ANCIENT ALLIANCE

FRIENDLY FIRE

In 1788 the people of this land were fire farmers. They made and maintained Australia by using fire and no fire to nourish and distribute plants, and plant distribution to locate animals, birds, reptiles and insects (hereafter animals). They made a plant community such as grass or open forest a favourable habitat, associated communities to link feed to shelter, and used associations to lure target animals. They put every species on ground it preferred, while they knew where resources were, and subject to Law could harvest them as they chose. They made paddocks without fences, possible because most Australian plants need or tolerate fire, and because there are few large native predators to disturb prey located by fire or no fire. They planned and worked hard to make plants and animals abundant, convenient and predictable. They depended not on chance, but on policy.

Newcomers could not imagine that policy. To them it defied common sense. Fire eats plants and litter, hardens ground and sterilises soil. In 1833 Charles Sturt concluded,

> The proportion of bad soil to ... good in New South Wales, is certainly very great ... the general want of vegetable mould over the colony [is due] chiefly to the ravages of ... [fire], whereby the growth of underwood, so favourable in other countries to the formation of soil, is wholly prevented ... There is no part of the world in which fires create such havoc as in ... Australia.[1]

In Tasmania botanist Ronald Campbell Gunn attributed

> the general poverty of the Soil ... to the habit the Aborigines had of regularly burning the Bush, thereby preventing that accumulation of decayed vegetable matter on the face of the Country, which would otherwise have necessarily occurred when the whole face of the Country is covered with wood.[2]

Yet Australia's plants thrived. Millennia before, fire and most plants had allied, letting both increase their range. About 70 per cent of Australia's plants either use fire to reseed or regenerate, or can recover from all but the hottest or most frequent fires. Most plants that need no fire are in rainforest or wetland where fire rarely thrives, but even wet forest mountain ash, for example, accepts infrequent fire. Fire and no fire shape the ecological arrangement of Australia.

Eucalypts greet fire with astonishing ingenuity. Their open branches, notorious for giving so little shade, channel fire up and out. Their thin leaves, rich in oil, especially in the south, wait to burn. You smell that oil best on a hot day: heat releases it. In other words, the leaves release highly flammable oil on days when it is most likely to catch alight. Many eucalypts also drop bark, again mostly in summer. It too is flammable, especially once dropped – colonial cooks used its sudden flare to bake cakes. How much bark a tree drops depends on the species, but generally the bigger the tree the more bark it drops. So in peak fire seasons these eucalypts drop a bark-fuel load adjusted to their size, thus encouraging fire while regulating its speed and intensity and removing competing understorey. Trunks resist fire, loose bark or ironbark corrugations shooting flames rapidly up. It scorches leaves and twigs, but trunk and branch sprout afresh, giving the tree an instant height advantage in the eternal competition for space and light.

Tropical eucalypts welcome fire much less than their southern cousins. They don't drop flammable bark, their leaves carry less oil, they don't hold seed for post-fire recovery, and few use buds or lignotubers (buds below ground), and those rarely. Yet they seem to expect what they usually get, frequent cool fires that suppress competitors without damaging crowns. They dominate the northern savanna. Everywhere fire promotes eucalypts, and eucalypts help fire spread. Together they have captured all but the wettest and driest parts of Australia.

Fire also generally favours species like banksias, callistemons and hakeas which grow and seed rapidly. Fire kills them but opens their hard pods, and they shed copious seed onto the rich ash beds they and fire have allied to lay down. Infrequent fire can let other plants smother such seedlings, much as eucalypts overtake wattles in time and block their light, but fire and rain free them. In arid zones seeds might wait decades, even centuries, for rain; elsewhere they crowd the land rapidly.

Acacias (wattles) range nearly all Australia and rule the inland. Most expect drought. They use little nutrient but chase moisture. A seedling's root can be four or five times its height, and it goes straight down: try transplanting one. Even so wattles are equipped to die, and in drought might die over many kilometres, seed beds dormant. Fire is drought with legs. Most wattles meet fire with their drought defences, with similar results. They die, but when conditions suit their seedlings quickly reoccupy the ground. The botanist Charles von Hügel saw this near Sydney in 1834, adding,

> The same appears to be the case with most of the seeds of plants classed as 'New Holland plants', which all grow in the arid soil along the coast or inland. These scrubs were subjected to regular firing by the Aborigines for so long that it would have been impossible for any plant to grow there without this characteristic.[3]

'New Holland plants' relate so closely to fire that it can group them. Species are fire avoiding, fire tolerant, fire dependent, fire promoting, fire sensitive (killed by fire but seeding after it) or fire intolerant (killed by fire).

Fire-avoiding plants thrive on no fire. Many perennial herbs and bulbs flourish in cool, wet months and die back in summer, so if fire comes roots or bulbs are below ground and only the surface stems burn off. No fire also restricts fire-tolerant plants. It lets fire-sensitive plants like mulga take over, and rainforest crowd under eucalypts and smother seedlings, so that after a long enough no-fire interval rainforest dominates.

Fire-dependent plants include some near the hottest (spinifex) and coldest (buttongrass) parts of Australia. Near both extremes, grasstree trunks resist fire but rot without it, and fire ash generates the wonderful flowerings of bulbs, lilies and orchids in the season after a big fire. Without fire shrubs and grasses smother these species before themselves becoming moribund, but suitably timed fires can trigger species to regenerate (daisy, bracken, bush tomato), sprout from lignotubers (banksia, tea-tree, heath), flower (Christmas bell, gymea lily, grasstree, waratah, daisy), germinate (heath, indigofera, hakea and others with hard seeds or pods), or die but set seed (mountain ash though not in cool fire, mulga, many central Australian shrubs), while fire ash provides nutrients (blady grass, bracken, heath) or activates soil bacteria to increase nutrient supply (cycad).

Most native grasses are perennial, drought-hardy and summer flourishing. On the Macintyre (NSW) during the 1827 drought botanist Allan Cunningham was 'surprised to observe how wonderfully the native grasses had resisted the dry weather ... They appeared fresh and nutritive, affording abundance of provision to the many kangaroos that were bounding around us.'[4] 'Nothing which I observed', William Morton wrote north-west of Rockhampton (Qld) in 1859,

> caused in me so much astonishment as the greenness of the grass. I had expected to see it all dried up by the heat of the tropical climate. At the beginning of September there had been no rain for four months, yet everywhere the grass was remarkably green, and became greener every week till I left in November.[5]

1788's most widespread perennial was kangaroo grass. Caviar to stock, it fed colonial Australia's prosperity. Its tussocks are grey-green year long, including summer, keeping soil damp, shielding against drought, offering feed when most needed. When burnt it comes back, and it needs a refreshing fire about every two to three years, whereas a northern perennial also refreshed by fire, Mitchell grass, is deterred by such frequent burning. Each responds to fire in its own way.

Curiously, 1788 Australia carried more grass and more open forest than it would have without fire, while sometimes plants that the land should have supported were not there. Near Kapunda (SA) this puzzled Edward Eyre:

> Forcing his way through dense, and apparently interminable scrub, formed by the Eucalyptus Dumosa [white mallee], (which

in some situations is known to extend for fully 100 miles), the traveller suddenly emerges into an open plain, sprinkled over with a fine silky grass, varying from a few acres to many thousands in extent, but surrounded on all sides by the dreary scrub he has left.[6]

In 1844 Sturt too found odd

the general appearance of the wooded portion of [South Australia] ... open forest without the slightest undergrowth save grass ... In many places the trees are so sparingly, and I had almost said judiciously distributed as to resemble the park lands attached to a gentleman's residence in England.[7]

Equally curious, plants with unlike fire responses were neighbours. Open forest clear of scrub gave way within a metre to dense forest and thick scrub, with no soil change. Grass burnt regularly edged rainforest never burnt. Tranquillity mintbush, a shrub of eucalypt rainforest boundaries, germinates best after low-intensity fire, neighbouring grass after medium-intensity fire, and neighbouring rainforest is killed by almost any fire, yet all were neighbours.[8] Blue cypress needs cool fire every two to eight years: more often or too hot kills it, less often chokes it with saplings, yet stands flourished amid fire-welcoming species.[9] Desert raisin (*Solanum*) dies without fire, but nearby foods can be either fire tolerant (bush banana, bush plum) or intolerant (fig, quandong). Mulga and gidgee die even in cool fire, and fires more than once a decade or so eradicate stands because no tree can flower in time, yet both grow among spinifex, which needs fire every three to five years to flourish. In heathland, too much fire creates sedgeland, too little creates woodland, yet heath banksia (*ericifolia*) needs fire to germinate but is discouraged if burnt more than every eight to ten years and killed if burnt every three to four years.[10] Tuning to such precise but erratic constraints should sooner or later have made most plant communities vulnerable, yet they flourished in 1788.

At Port Lincoln (SA) Thomas Allen, 'late Gardener to His Majesty William the Fourth at Kew', glimpsed why. He saw trees burnt away to leave the best soil to grass:

> the native fires that so destructively take place on the best land of the greatest vegetative qualities ... forms the truest and most certain criterion of the goodness of the soil; as when land is seen quite bare, from burning, is positive proof to a practical observer that the soil is of first-rate quality, but which to a superficial observer, ignorant of the circumstances and cause, would absolutely consider the best land to be a comparative desert, and unfit for cultivation.[11]

Where plants were was no fluke. Fire needs plants for fuel, plants need fire or no fire to thrive, but their alliance needs a spark. Lightning provides this sometimes, but erratically, and even today is uncommon, letting fuel build up for years before it strikes. In 1788 it sparked even fewer fires because there was less fuel.

Why was there less fuel? Because people held the spark. This gave them opportunity and purpose. They joined the plant–fire alliance then went further, using fire to work the land as intimately as humans can. They learnt which plants to burn, when, how often and how hot, maintaining country in more complex mosaics than random fire possibly could. Selecting where plants grew let them locate where animals went. Holding the spark let them shape their world.

PROTECTING

They protected plants from unsuitable fire. In Tasmania fire kills species like beech, King Billy pine and pencil pine, yet 2000-year-old trees flourished. In the Centre native bees prefer desert bloodwood, so people take care not to let flames or smoke damage its flowers. Everywhere cool fire averted hot fire and avoided damaging flowers, fruit, nuts and seed, while people backburnt around special places and tree clumps to make them safe. Spirits live in such places and blind with smoke anyone who lights a fire too close.

Plants compete: protecting plants required balance. For example people must choose whether to burn grass to expose yams, or wait till the same grass ripens into grain. In wet country people preferred the yams, in dry the grain.

HELPING

Helping plants and animals was a major responsibility. From rainforest to spinifex, plants were patch-burnt to ensure refuges, vary habitats, and make diverse-rich edges. 'The burning of country was not at all random', Dick Kimber noted of the Centre,

> there was greater attention to areas favoured by certain nutritious or otherwise useful plants and to areas favoured by certain animals. A patchy mosaic of vegetation in different stages of regeneration ... almost completely eliminated the risk of large scale wildfires ... the fired lower slopes of the George Gill Range promoted the flourishing growth of highly prized native or bush tobacco, while in the Tanami and Sandy Deserts burning promoted the growth of two kinds of sweet-tasting solanum.[12]

Bush tobacco (pituri) and some solanum are annuals: they burn readily. Yet such 'fire-weeds' commonly grew near fire-sensitive mulga and fire-dependent spinifex. Only precise and timely fire and no fire could balance such diverse plant preferences so neatly.

People helped crop plants by destroying competition. Cycad nuts (zamia) are poisonous: eating them raw nearly killed Ludwig Leichhardt's party on its way to Port Essington (NT) in 1845. Yet once the poison is leached out the nuts are highly nutritious, so people made cycad gardens. They burnt away competing plants and timed their fires to increase nut production and synchronise nut maturity, creating predictable harvests that let them gather for ceremony.

Locating plants located animals. At Albany (WA) George Vancouver observed in 1791, 'Fire is frequently resorted to by rude nations, either for the purpose of encouraging a sweeter growth of herbage in their hunting grounds, or as tools for taking the wild animals, of which they are in pursuit.'[13] This meant not merely burning the grass, but making it grassland in the first place, perhaps generations before (see 'Templates' in Chapter 7). In north-west Tasmania Henry Hellyer remarked in 1828, 'It is possible that the natives by burning only one set of plains are enabled to keep the kangaroos more concentrated for their use, and I can in no way account for their burning only in this place, unless it is to serve them as a hunting place.'[14] Aboriginal people themselves stated at Evans Bay (Qld) in 1849, 'observing that the grass had been burnt on portions of the flats the Blacks said that the rain that was coming on would make the young grass spring up and that would bring down the kangaroos and the Blacks would spear them from the scrub'.[15] Evans Bay is next to Torres Strait, as far from Albany and Tasmania as you can get in Australia, yet all three peoples managed land similarly.

They fire-farmed. Prehistorian Rhys Jones coined 'fire-stick farming' to describe patch-burning grass to bring on green pick to lure grazing animals,[16] commonly kangaroos. To fire-farm them you must ensure that they go where you've burnt. So you must make sure the grass you burn is the sweetest and most nutritious available, provide shelter nearby so kangaroos won't feel vulnerable, and not burn other good grass too close.

The best grass is on the best soil. Trees grow there, so you must burn to keep the land more or less clear, yet leave belts of shelter trees neither too open so kangaroos feel exposed, nor too dense so they fear being slowed down. So you must make not only the grass but the land around, using at least three distinct fire regimes. No wonder totems embraced not only a plant or animal, but also its habitat.

Naturally, the survivors of a hunted mob move. People could not let that happen haphazardly, because the point of locating animals was to know where they were – to make them convenient and predictable. You must lure them to the next place you've prepared, then the next, and so on. In short you must pattern kangaroo country into places that will and won't attract them. Mac Core, a Cape York grazier born about 1915, said that when he was young, people broke the bush into plains about every 3–4 miles (5–6 kilometres), because that's how far roos there go when frightened. People lit a plain or two, waited till green pick lured the roos, then harvested what they needed. The rest would flee to nearby plains recently burnt, green pick just coming on ... and so on.[17] The animals were herded from one predictable site to another.

Early newcomers too noted kangaroos not continuously, but in mobs a few days apart. South-east of Tambo (Qld), Thomas Mitchell

> traversed fine open grassy plains. The air was fragrant from the many flowers then springing up, especially where the natives had burnt the grass ... The extensive burning of the natives, a work of considerable labour, and performed in dry warm weather, left tracts in the open forest, which had become green as an emerald with the young crop of grass. These plains were thickly imprinted with the feet of kangaroos, and the work is undertaken by the natives to attract these animals to such places.[18]

'Kangaroo Ground' remains a place name today.

'Fire-stick farming' was but one fire of many. It was an endpoint, a harvest fire on ground other fires made ready long before, perhaps including those hot fires so hard to control but so essential to regenerate some plant species or to hunt in season. People might also backburn around camps or clumps or single trees to protect them, or sheet-burn to clean country, or hot-burn to promote scrub to shelter small birds, or not burn to make forest or protect a vulnerable species, and so on. To think 'fire-stick farming' all people did is like confusing burning sugarcane with farming sugar.

REFRESHING

On several southern mallee and gum species people promoted a scale insect, lerp. Lerps make a sweet manna, and people burnt their trees to promote fresh leaves to feed them, then harvested the manna next year. 'There were bags full of it in almost every camp', Edward Curr recalled of the Lake Boga (Vic) district. He thought it a delicacy.[19]

People moved entire plant communities to refresh them. If silicon builds up in grass, grazers abandon it. Geographers Bob Ellis and Ian Thomas described Paradise Plains, near Mathinna (Tas). The Plains lie west–east; the prevailing winter wind is westerly. West to east, Ellis and Thomas found charred rainforest and eucalypt logs more than 200 years old under secondary rainforest, then eucalypt forest becoming progressively younger, then acacias, then grass, then mature rainforest. Tasmanians had used westerlies to drive grass fires into rainforest at the eastern edge. Were this all it might be random, but people did not want grass plains too big, nor to destroy too much eucalypt forest or rainforest, for they too were habitats. They used no fire as a tool, taking care to leave the western eucalypt edge unburnt. This let eucalypts there regenerate and advance east, then let rainforest follow under their shelter to reclaim the ground. Thus over centuries people progressively moved grass, eucalypts and rainforest from west to east. Ellis and Thomas noted similar landscapes at Diddleum Plain and near Mount Maurice, and Bill Mollison saw them in north-west Tasmania, using hot summer northerlies.[20]

SUPPRESSING

> Fire, grass, kangaroos, and human inhabitants seem all dependent on each other for existence in Australia; for any one of these being wanting, the others could no longer continue. Fire is necessary to burn the grass, and form ... open forests ... [it] discloses vermin, birds' nests, &c, on which the females and children, who chiefly burn the grass, feed. But for this simple process, the Australian woods had probably continued as thick a jungle as those of New Zealand or America.[21]

Suppressing meant balancing. Animals were culled if their numbers swelled off their totem places (see Chapter 5) – kangaroos were driven over cliffs for example. People also thinned or cleared trees for grass, removed scrub to open an understorey, burnt grass to reveal food plants. In Tasmania and along the mainland east coast they made the most extreme plant community conversion – rainforest to grass. Often that land is now rainforest again.

Fire suppressed insects. In 1802 François Péron thought it worth remark if he met insects in number, and near Parramatta went into forests

> into which the English had not yet gone with either implement or fire, and we observed that the insects are much less common there than in the areas already cleared by Europeans. This odd situation seemed to us to arise from the natives' practice of setting fire to the forests, thereby destroying a vast number of insect eggs and larvae and even fully developed insects.[22]

South of Sydney in 1826, Dumont d'Urville found plants and insects scarcer than he expected, 'due in great part to the frequent burning off carried out by the natives, which every year must kill off many species'.[23] Near Adelaide in 1841 Johannes Menge noted that fire permitted 'the retention within bounds of insect life (notably of the locust, grasshopper, caterpillar, ant and moth) ... and the comparative scarcity of insectivorous birds and birds of prey'.[24] The observant naturalist Alfred Howitt reported of Gippsland, 'The influence of these bush fires acted ... as a check upon insect life.'[25] In West Australian tuart forest fire controlled the tuart bud weevil, and in the Centre Ernest Giles remarked, 'Reptiles and insects ... are scarce, on account of the continual fires the natives use in their perpetual hunt for food.'[26] Timely fire may explain the seeming absence in 1788 of the Biblical-scale insect plagues grain farmers periodically suffer now.

DISTRIBUTING

Such facility with fire and no fire allowed people to distribute plants within their Country with the ease of a gardener, including putting fire-tolerant and fire-sensitive plants next to each other.

Distributing plants distributed animals, prey and predators alike, making them abundant, convenient, and predictable. What animals prefer always attracts them. Kangaroos crowd onto golf greens. They don't need to, they prefer to. For short, fresh grass they defy flying golf balls and angry greenkeepers when safer grass is metres away. Koalas prefer fresh tips, so fire can lure them to regenerating eucalypts. Possums too prefer fresh tips, so move readily from unburnt urban parks and fringes into green-laden backyards. Most animals prefer particular shelter: euros rocky hills, koalas tall eucalypts, scrub wallabies and small birds thick growth. Even scavengers have preferences. Emus eat grain, tips, flowers, insects, mice and small lizards but prefer fruit, so such adaptable opportunists can still be attracted.

Two key principles lay under this 'systematic management', as Leichhardt called it:[27]

1. Every species must be made abundant yet kept in balance with every other species, including us. The world was not made just for humans. That's the point of totems: they create specialists in understanding and protecting a species and its habitat.
2. Fire is an ally, but it must be managed. It was 1788's hardest and most constant work. No matter what the local conditions, people everywhere worked with fire and no fire to make

country abundant, predictable, useful and beautiful. Fire united Australia ecologically.

Some fires were for people. 'All tribes of natives appear to dread evil spirits', Eyre wrote,

> They fly about at nights through the air, break down branches of trees, pass simultaneously from one place to another, and attack all natives that come in their way, dragging such as they can after them. Fire appears to have considerable effect in keeping these monsters away, and a native will rarely stir a yard by night, except in moonlight, without carrying a fire-stick.[28]

People also burnt to clear tracks. Coastal grass or open forest corridors were common. One ran the length of the east coast, another around Tasmania, where people cleared forest and heath with fire but stopped the flames entering tree clumps. Newcomers there easily walked distances in a day impossible in today's dense forest. Other human purposes were to clean camps of litter, snakes, ants and mosquitoes, protect special places, harvest, hunt or make ground ready to hunt, care for water edges, signal, teach, and assure neighbours and ancestors that country is being properly cared for. If people don't see smoke where it should be, they assume something is wrong, and look to see what it is.

Fire led people to resolutely mobile lives so that all land was managed. It was built into hearts and minds. Yanyuwa (NT) people have single words for 'badly burnt country', 'well-burnt country, good to hunt on', and 'lighting small fires in a row, to burn a beach front or a large plain'.[29] West Arnhem people have phrases for 'low, creeping fires' and for 'cleaning the country' with hot fires.[30] Arnhem Land plateau people link bushfire, the mid-Dry peak fire season and in some dialects burnable grass with the same stem word, *wurrk*.[31] Martu (WA) people say *nyurnma* for a freshly burnt area, *waru-waru* for the green-shoot time after fire, *mukura* for the growth flush one to three years later, and *mangul* when spinifex begins to dominate country five to seven years later.[32] East of Perth in the 1830s people had one word for every stage of a burn: 'ground clothed with vegetation which has not yet been burned', 'unburned ground, but ready for burning. Land of which the vegetation is abundant and dry, fit to be set on fire', 'ground where vegetation has been burnt', 'burned ground', and 'young grass springing up after the country has been burned ... the seed of any plant'. None of these words have an English equivalent; none describe random fire. Most striking, east of Perth *kalla* meant 'fire; a fire; (figuratively) an individual's district; a property in land'.[33] *Kalla* equated fire with Country.

This changed the nature of fire and the nature of Australia. A constant spark changed the dominant fire from infrequent and hot to common and cool. This favoured some plants and suppressed others, changing the face of the land. Land naturally treed became grass, dense forest and rainforest became open forest, forest became plant mosaics. In arid country annual food plants occupy ground that without fire would be spinifex. At the other extreme, almost all Tasmania is naturally rainforest, but it is rare in the east and spattered with tussock or heath land in the west.

Despite such myriad local variation, from spinifex to rainforest the basic purposes of fire and no fire were the same: to ensure diversity and abundance, to regulate plant and animal populations, to leave the world as the ancestors made it. The plant patterns people made with fire were the same too: grass on good soil, forest split by grass, tree and scrub clumps in grassland, undergrowth uncommon. And the benefits were the same: plants and animals were located comfortably, conveniently and predictably.

How were such sweeping continental innovations possible?

7

HOLDING THE SPARK

HOW TO BURN

Fire and people shared a special alliance. Only they were free of ecological restraint; only they ranged across land and totem. Everything else had habitats. From an early age people studied fire, and fire totem people devoted their lives to it. They worked harder at fire than at any other task. When conditions suited, hardly a day passed without a fire being lit somewhere, always according to Law, always planned and predictable. Fire became scalpel more than sword, sustaining more diversity than any natural regime could conceivably maintain, taming the most fire-prone continent on earth, giving Country the kiss of life.

Fire was planned. Guided by experts, ancestors and neighbours, elders would discuss what, when and how to burn. 'What must be made absolutely clear, is that the rules for fire and fire use are many and varied, and are dependent upon an intimate knowledge of the physical and spiritual nature of each portion of the land.'[1] Hard-won local expertise blended with knowing fire as a living part of the Dreaming, subject to Law via ceremony.

Fire began with ceremony. In summer in south-west Australia, people went burning 'in all directions', but only after several nights of *man carl* (bushfire) ceremony.[2] In Tomkinson River country near Maningrida (NT),

> children learn about fire from their parents and being told stories about who can make fires, different types of burning and the responsibilities of *djungkay* [ceremonial managers], the people who help the landowners look after the country and our law. Responsibilities depend on a person's relationship to the landowners of a particular estate.[3]

Nothing but the correct rituals done at the right time by the right people made things work. 'You sing the country before you burn it. In your mind you see the fire, you know where it is going, and you know where it will stop. Only then do you light the fire.'[4] People know how a correct fire behaves, but it does so because they have performed the correct ceremonies. What seems casual burning depends on knowing intimately the land and its songs.

This rough table omits no fire, has too few categories and doesn't locate animals, but it helps convey the subtlety and control of 1788 fire.

MANAGEMENT FIRES

TYPE	PURPOSE	WHERE
Burn early and often:		
Small, cool. Damp, cool times. Planned.	Protect camps, special places, water, fire-sensitive plants.	See 'Purpose'. Edges.
Follow the drying land 1:		
Small to more extensive, cool, frequent. Planned.	Fire breaks, patches, firestick farm, freshen grass, protect conservation areas/special places, clearings.	Grass, annuals, woodland. Edges, clearings.
Follow the drying land 2:		
Bigger, cool, frequent. Planned.	Firestick farm, make patches, clear seedlings and scrub, promote or balance habitats, chance to hunt especially small game.	Grass, woodland, forest, scrub, rock country, reeds?
Finish country:		
Cool, perhaps hot, confined. Often in summer. Planned.	Expose food, germinate plants (fire and smoke), extend patches, chance to hunt.	Long grass, scrub, trees, rocky hills. Bulbs and tubers, mangroves? heath?

TYPE	PURPOSE	WHERE
Clean-up:		
Hot, extensive. Uncommon. Summer, late Dry. Planned.	Clean dirty country, clear trees, clear melaleuca, germinate scrub, chance to hunt.	More common in open country; wet forest and rainforest very rarely.
Unplanned??		
War, lightning.		

Most land was not burnt every year, but every corner of the continent was cared for. People burnt the most useful land most and sterile or sensitive land perhaps not for generations, but there was no wilderness in 1788 – we brought that. Fire was the essential ally in civilising the continent.

CONTROL

Whoever lit a fire, even a campfire, was responsible for it. Random fire, however begun, was an offence. It defied the logic of templates (see p. 123). It could damage a template but not repair it. It could make clumps and patches and edges but not sustain them. It made animals disperse unpredictably, for animals have no fire defence save flight or going underground. It was never welcome. System and precision were its enemies. All today's big bushfires are random fires.

To control fire, people usually burnt coolly and patchily to break a potential fire front, aimed their fires at water or rock or burnt ground, patrolled edges, kept fire out of canopies, used wind to turn fire back on itself, and predicted dew at night. South of Mount Barker (WA) in the 1830s, John Lort Stokes

> met a party of natives engaged in burning the bush, which they do in sections every year. The dexterity with which they manage so proverbially a dangerous agent as fire is indeed astonishing. Those to whom this duty is especially entrusted, and who guide or stop the running flame, are armed with large green boughs, with which, if it moves in the wrong direction, they beat it out ... I can conceive no finer subject for a picture than a party of these swarthy beings engaged in kindling, moderating, and directing the destructive element, which under their care seems almost to change its nature, acquiring, as it were, complete docility, instead of the ungovernable fury we are accustomed to ascribe to it.[5]

Such skills are for docile fire only. They are largely useless against today's infernos. They assume that random fire never takes hold.

Uluru elders explained how intricately connected fire and Country were:

> The country is not burnt in just any way. *Anungu* [Anangu] are taught by their grandparents the proper way to burn, according to the *Tjukurpa* [Dreaming]. Certain places, such as sacred sites and trees such as fig trees, should not be burnt because of their associations with the *Tjukurpa*. The area around these trees is often burned to protect them ... and show others that the land is being properly cared for.

> Burning of spinifex – the rubbish stuff – and sometimes mulga, helps grow food for animals and people and makes it easier to walk around the place. *Mingkiri* [small marsupials] and many of the larger animals like the country being burned because they eat the same seeds and things as *Anungu* and get plenty of food when it starts growing again.
>
> The *Tjukurpa* shows *Anungu* how animals will be with fire and burnt country. For example, some dragon lizards and other small animals don't like the ground after it's been burnt. They go away for a while, and then come back when the spinifex has grown again. Some animals, such as the spinifex hopping-mouse, like it both ways. They move into the burned areas to feed and then return to safety in the large unburnt spinifex hummocks where they have their burrows. *Kalaya* and *malu* (emu and kangaroo) do not like freshly burnt country but come back to it after rain has put on the green feed. Most animals and birds love the green feed near water.[6]

The key components of fire control are frequency and timing (year, season, day), intensity, and patchiness.

FIRE FREQUENCY AND TIMING: YEAR

The marks of fire were so common that early newcomers wrongly assumed that people burnt everywhere every year. Thomas Mitchell observed in 1836,

> the trees and shrubs being very inflammable, conflagrations take place so frequently and intensively, in the woods during summer, as to leave very little vegetable matter to return to earth. On the highest mountains, and in places the most remote and desolate, I have always found on every dead trunk on the ground, and living tree of any magnitude also, the marks of fire; and thus it appears that these annual conflagrations extend to every place.[7]

Fire frequency varied in tune with plant preferences. Apart from fire-sensitive plants rarely burnt, it could range from twice a year for grass to one to four years for grass, annuals, tree seedlings and rainforest edges and clearings, two to four for grass and open forest, three to five to control scrub and ten to twenty-five to promote it, seven for high-altitude forest, ten to twenty for coastal heath, and decades or centuries for wet eucalypt forest and rainforest, all these rough generalisations being modified by local circumstance.

Overall, people burnt more ground more often than newcomers today, but less fuel. Frequency and fuel parried one another. Infrequent fire commonly made trees and scrub, frequent fire commonly made grass. Grassland was more common in 1788 than now, and much more common than it would have been without 1788 fire. In high-country eucalypt forest near Canberra, John Banks did find fire less common before settlers arrived than after, but it is a question whether 1788 cool fires left any burn mark he could measure. More frequent 1788 patch fires are implied by his finding that 'the original forest consisted largely of uneven-aged stands of older, widely spaced trees ... Today this picture has been reversed, with dense even-aged stands – typically dating from major fires in the 1880s, early 1900s, 1926 or 1939 – dominating the forest.'[8]

FIRE FREQUENCY AND TIMING: SEASON

The best time to burn is before rain, even though rain disperses animals, and people too, as then they can use dry country or venture far into desert, leaving more permanent water for drought times. Fire before rain promotes grass, annuals, fruit, seed and animal breeding. Near Clermont (Qld) in 1862, the plains

> had evidently been burnt before this late rain by the blacks, and ... were clothed with a carpet of burnt feed, forming a vivid green dotted with a variety of wild flowers, also many kinds of wild peas and vetches, wild cucumbers, and other trailing plants ... Never after ... did I see it in such splendid condition – I might, indeed, say glory.[9]

To predict rain, people watched animal behaviour: ants moving eggs to higher ground, birds seeking shelter and so on. You can also smell rain coming.

The next best time to burn is after rain.

> The natives had burnt all the grass at Gippsland late in summer. Heavy rains must have fallen before we reached there, in the month of March ... The whole country was very green. It had here

the appearance of young cornfields; the young grass was about six inches high, and in places very thick.[10]

Opportunistic burning before or after rain, still controlled, could cut across a seasonal fire program.

Otherwise, south to north the peak fire season broadly moved from summer to autumn to winter and the Dry, although in desert the time of year was less important than when rain fell. People rarely burnt in spring as this threatened young plants and animals and was a good time to hunt kangaroos and emus which flee from fire.

In higher rainfall regions in the south-west and south-east including Tasmania, people burnt from summer into autumn, peaking in mid-summer on the mainland south coast to late summer further north. Around Sydney people preferably burnt after late spring or early summer rain.[11] More precise timing depended on what people were burning for. At Albany (WA) burning began in summer when animals were old enough to evade fire, around Perth autumn burns promoted herbs, winter and early spring burns promoted shrubs. Burning grass in early summer exposed tubers for harvest; mid to late summer burns waited until tubers seeded and became dormant; autumn burns cleared grain stubble after harvest.

In southern Queensland fire peaked in late autumn and winter, while in the Centre people burnt in winter but sometimes in summer, depending on their purpose. At Amata (SA) Frank Young, a senior fire man, said that people burn mainly in the cold time, and stop when the winds start about August. First they burn around sites needing protection. These might vary from year to year: in 2002 there was concern for dragon lizards, so their sites were burnt around early with cool fires. People next burn over the country, taking care to burn downwind of sensitive plants like mulga, desert oak and witchetty bush, especially as these are scarcer since the cattle times. People burn at cooler times, early morning or late afternoon, depending on how far the fire must go. These fires create patches and soon burn out because the spinifex is green – even old man spinifex is green at its base and damp under it. If a fire does trickle on, night dews in this cold time put it out.[12] Martu people (WA) too burn mostly in winter, as strong winds then mean a fire burns out relatively quickly into a downwind firebreak.[13]

A little further north, people burnt most in summer, preferably before rain tailing down from the northern Wet. On a hot day in October 1872, Ernest Giles saw men burning extensively west of the MacDonnell Ranges,[14] and Walter Smith Purula, a southern Aranda (now Arrernte) elder, told his friend Dick Kimber, 'You can't burn wrong time, like, summer time it's got to be burnt, but no good winter time. They die. All them tucker trees ... But if they burn them summer time and a storm comes, it grows lovely.'[15] Yet in winter people might burn after rain, though not in frost because fire won't travel then.

The fire season peaks later as it moves north from desert to higher rainfall areas. In south Kimberley it is from February to August; in north Kimberley from May to October.[16] Cape York people burn little after about August, to protect rainforest edges and their yams. Arnhem Land plateau people start burning about mid-Dry; elsewhere fires start in the late Wet. While there is still some rain and fuel and ground are damp, people burn small patches that soon go out, but that make mini-firebreaks for later Dry season burns. In the south we say you can't burn when it's wet, but in the north that's when they start. On the coast near Borroloola (NT), Yanyuwa elder Musso Harvey explained,

> You got to burn the country ... not leave him till he really dry, that means you destroy everything ... cook it ... Soon as wet season stop ... grass starting to dry out, you burn grass then ... so you don't burn all the animals ... if you burn it [then,] some have a place to hide, but if you leave him, and you burn the grass you kill everything, that's no good.[17]

People burn first round camps, lagoons and special places, then throughout the Dry they chase the drying land with firesticks, beginning on plains, next forest, then rock and plateau country, finally water edges not burnt in the late Wet. They burn somewhere almost every day, especially with dew, mostly in mosaics, peaking about mid-Dry. The hottest fires are in the late Dry, aimed into grass country already patch-burnt. As the next Wet nears they might burn into forest understorey depending on the plants and creatures in it, and they keep burning into the early Wet as chances arise. Fire is with them constantly. Annual grass burns make months of smoke and kilometres of burnt ground, but that's how it is in the north. People endure but few complain, not even whitefellas in Darwin. They know that controlled fire keeps them safe.

FIRE TIMING: DAY

The right time of day to burn hinges on knowing such a myriad of changing interactions of climate, plant and animal that it can only be done well locally, where each family knows its own ground intimately. Before lighting a fire for example, people might predict how much dew is needed to put it out. This is very local knowledge, yet some general skills apply.

You can tell by feel if it's time to burn a perennial grass. If it feels powdery it will collapse before the flame and a fire will stutter out, or at best travel slowly. If the stems are juicy, if they bend at the touch, this fire too will at best get going slowly. If the stems snap, they're right to burn. Or more exactly they might be. It depends why you are burning. If you want to burn grassland belonging to a grass wren or a skink totem, you might burn when the grass is not ideal for it, so that such creatures find easier refuge. In breeding or flower seasons you would not normally burn even if the grass is suitable for it. If you are building up food to host a big ceremony you might burn differently. Fire is adjusted to circumstance, as seasons vary, rain is erratic, plants have life cycles, animals populate unevenly, fire has long- and short-term effects, and people differ on what to favour.

INTENSITY

Frequency and intensity dance in tandem: more of one means less of the other. Over the same ground, frequent fires are cool fires, by far the most important fire type. They destroy less, promote plants, make patches, put feed next to shelter, and are easy to control. In Victoria in 1842 a Scottish visitor remarked that grass fires were

> common during the summer ... The flames came on at a slow pace ... as the grass happened to be short, the fiery line seldom rose above the fuel on which it fed; and it would have been no difficult matter to have leapt across it ... The frequency of these fires is the principal cause of the absence of underwood, that renders the forest so pervious in all directions, and gives to Australia the park-like appearance which all agree in considering its characteristic feature.[18]

Yet persistent cool fire caused a slow decline in the lowland grass wren in West Australian heathland, and threatens mallee fowl.[19] Since hot fire also endangers these birds, fine-tuned burning based on detailed local knowledge is crucial.

On Cape York, Kuku Thaypan elders warn that, among other effects, a fire that scorches canopies thereby kills flowers, reducing seeds, nectar and pollen for insects, in turn disadvantaging insectivorous birds and nectar eaters such as small marsupials and bats. The same fire causes excessive leaf drop which increases fuel loads and might smother grass, cause bare ground, and heat soil, affecting germination.[20] Yet newcomers think such a fire quite mild. We don't merely scorch canopies, we incinerate them.

Fire leaves burnt and unburnt patches, the hotter the fire the fewer and smaller the unburnt patches. Hot fires were uncommon but sometimes necessary – for example to regenerate scrub, clean country, or summer-burn melaleuca thickets every 25–30 years for tammar wallaby habitat.[21] In dry country in the morning or at dusk, people lit sheet-burns, firing long reaches of country, but even then they put out fires that threatened to get away, and buried burning fallen trees because wind can 'chuck the coals a long way'.[22] Such practices 'almost completely eliminated the risk of large scale wildfires'.[23] Sheet-burns were aimed at big unburnt patches in late summer in the south and late Dry in the north, in strong wind and often in the heat of the day, making the belts of angry flame and surging smoke that photographers love. Yet wind-driven fires move quickly and canopies were rarely burnt. In the north whirlwinds take ash from such fires hundreds of metres into the sky: this is the Rainbow Serpent going up to start another Wet. 'The Rainbow is burning', Yanyuwa people say: their word for 'whirlwind', 'cyclone', 'rainbow serpent' and some snakes is the same: *bugimala*.[24]

Fire alarmed newcomers. At home they saw fire mostly in fireplaces: Australian fires awed them. Yet most were much milder than today's firestorms. Above Hobart in January 1802, François Péron reported,

> on all sides the forests were on fire. Their savage inhabitants ... had withdrawn to a lofty mountain, which itself looked like a huge pyramid of flame and smoke ... the fire had destroyed all the grass, and most of the bushes and small trees had met with the same fate; the largest trees were blackened almost to their summits, and in some places had fallen under the violence of the flames and huge blazing heaps had been formed of their remains.

Yet Péron followed the fire up the mountain, walking into it in places and finding unburnt huts at the summit, and next day the fire was out.[25]

At Adelaide, Mary Thomas wrote of Kaurna people,

> The greatest mischief they have ... is a custom of burning the grass during the hot weather ... Their fires on the hills are quite awful. We have frequently seen fires this summer which have reached for twenty or thirty miles in circumference, for they light them at distances so that they will enclose a large space,[26]

and in 1844 George French Angas similarly described the Adelaide Hills:

> They consist of tall primeval trees of a kind of eucalyptus, their erect and massive trunks blackened, in many places as high as fifteen or twenty feet from the ground, by the tremendous fires that sweep through these forests, and continue to blaze and roll along, day and night for many miles, in one continuous chain of fire. These conflagrations usually take place during the dry heats of summer, and frequently at night; the hills, when viewed from Adelaide, present a singular and almost terrific appearance; being covered with long streaks of flame, so that one might fancy them a range of volcanoes.[27]

In such mature forest, fire 'fifteen or twenty feet from the ground' (4.5 to 6 metres) would not be thought big today, and in those same hills three years before Angas a reporter observed,

> though the fire has evidently ranged fiercely in many places, yet it never seems to attack anything but the grass and the leaves of the lower bushes, leaving the trees unscathed, the larger ones being seldom found hollow and blackened as are those on the plains below.[28]

At Albany in 1830, Scott Nind noted, 'The violence of the fire is frequently very great, and extends over many miles of country; but this is generally guarded against by their burning it in consecutive portions.'[29] Clearly this refers to controlled fire – hardly violent by 2021 standards.

Given such control, did people burn to hunt, or hunt when they burnt? Small fires for small game apart, which women lit as they walked along, random fire disperses animals and damages plants unpredictably, so fire must be planned and predictable. On the north-west Kimberley coast in the 1920s,

> the men welcome the time when the grass is dry enough to burn. They will decide ... what spot they will choose for the next burning party. These are exciting expeditions, in which all the men take part. Early on the morning of the burning the men will be seen rubbing and painting their bodies with white clay. Soon after sunrise they will muster, carrying their weapons, and go through a performance that might be called a dance.

Then they go off, some to burn, some to hunt.[30] This seems a hunt organised when it was time to burn.

Hunting at least respected proper burn times. In Arnhem Land,

> Grass is not fired at random but in limited areas always held under control ... The burning of the grass, although it yields much animal food, has the disadvantage of destroying the vines of food plants and so is carried out with great care until the vegetable harvest is well advanced.[31]

On Cape York too the castaway Narcisse Pelletier described 'the care the savages take in firing the woods where the yams grow so that the tubers of these plants develop more extensively and their crop is more plentiful'.[32]

So probably people hunted when they burnt, not the reverse, not randomly. A Yolŋu (NT) elder explained,

> 'Burn grass time' gives us good hunting. It brings animals such as wallabies, kangaroos and turkeys on the fresh new feed of green grasses and plants. But it does not only provide for us but also for animals, birds, reptiles and insects. After the 'burn' you will see hundreds of white cockatoos digging for grass roots ... If it wasn't burnt they would not be able to penetrate the dense and long speargrass and other grasses for these sources of food.[33]

TEMPLATES

Templates were the land's finishing touches: mosaics of tree or scrub belts and clumps, grass clearings and corridors, unlike plants alternating, all with diverse-rich edges, purposefully distributed. By creating optimum conditions on templates and not nearby, people made target plants and animals on them abundant, convenient, and predictable. Typically they chose a feature like water, hill or rock, and with cool fire and no fire laid out a template nearby. No matter which plants dominated locally, similar templates for similar purposes recurred across Australia. To associate food or feed plants with shelter plants for example, grass might separate forest from water, tree belts channel a plain, young and old spinifex alternate, clearings spatter rainforest. Each rotated growth in planned sequences, some to harvest, some to locate.

In the Centre in 1876 the poet James Grassie noticed a template in range and variety unlike any other newcomers reported:

> remarkable ... in the Mallee territory, and thence to the vicinity of Cooper's Creek, is the rapidity with which the vegetation changes, and the straight lines each class maintains, running close and parallel to other classes. One sand rise, for instance, is clothed with pine trees, while the next at a few yards distance has only Mallee bushes, a third porcupine grass [spinifex], and a fourth salt bush, the whole growing out of pure sand apparently of the same deposit. On one sand rise you see ... quondongs, and all at once you enter an enormous garden of hops all-ready for picking. From

the hops you emerge upon a vast plain of pig faces, from the pig faces to salt bush, and from the salt bush to heath or scrub, and so on during the whole route. The pine will run close to the Mallee for miles as straight as an arrow, and the other vegetation seems to be all separate and in well defined paddocks – each paddock being as large as a dozen of German principalities.[34]

The map opposite shows another precise template in south-west New South Wales. Along survey lines at top left, and presumably off them too, pine and grey-box clumps run west–east and north–south roughly a kilometre apart; at centre similarly spaced plains sit in trees; elsewhere thin tree lines circle saltbush and grass plains. About 1842 Edward Curr similarly described adjoining country east and as far as 60 miles (96 kilometres) south of the Murray, which he said people burnt.[35] In 2012 David Joss of Mathoura (NSW) wrote, 'I have had this map for some years and puzzled over the swiss-cheese patterns.' The landowner was 'not aware of any major differences in soil types which might cause trees to grow in such a way'.[36] Careful fire made this country. In Tasmania George Robinson noted equally precise templates for animals: 'inland natives have their hunting grounds for the different species of game, i.e. boomer, forester, wallaby, kangaroo, wombat, porcupine &c'.[37]

Such templates could be close, but when activated with fire had to be far enough apart not to disrupt each other, as this would make target animals unpredictable and the system pointless. Activating a template thus meant talking to neighbours and elders. The Law prescribed most of this, but still negotiation must have been frequent,

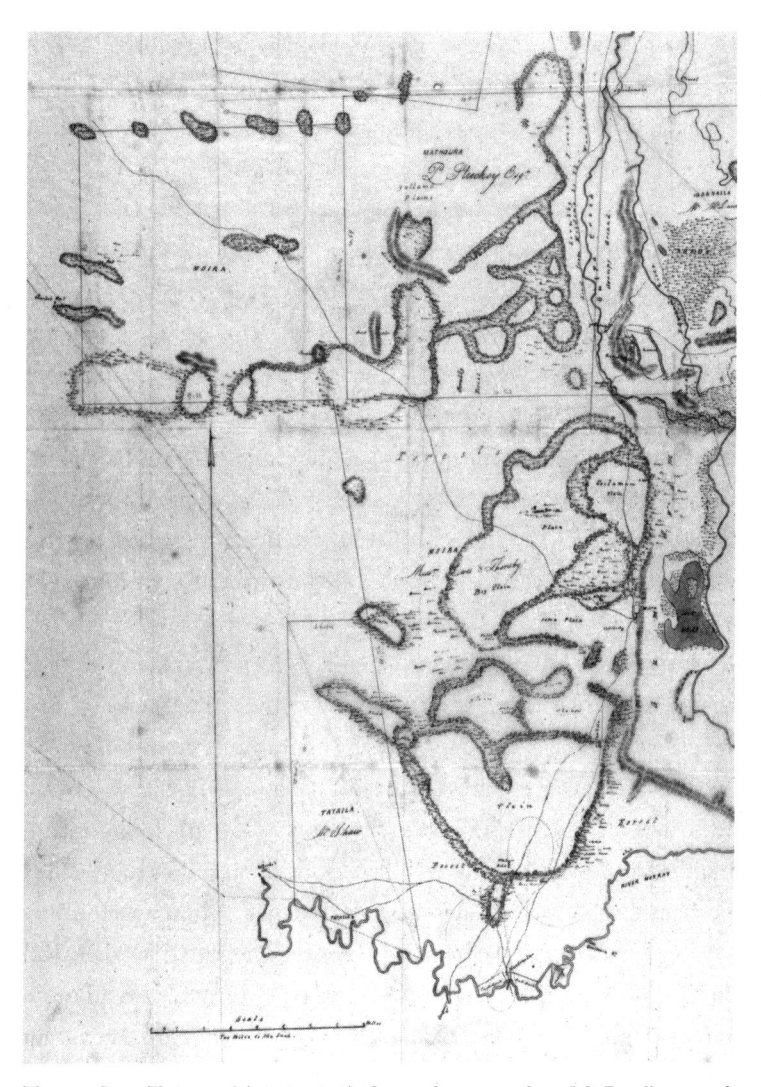

Thomas Scott Townsend (1812–1869), Copy of a tracing from Mr Boyd's map of the Edward and Murray rivers country, 1848 (detail).

so the template system could hardly have had land boundaries. There could not be a place where it was practised next to a place where it wasn't; a place where neighbours negotiated habitually next to a place where they behaved randomly. Australia was inexorably a single estate.

Dirty country undermined templates. This happened when a community was decimated by death or deportation. Scrub thickening, grass matted or rotting, trees invading grassland, litter building up, insects and snakes abounding provoked grief and shame. Even distant neighbours could see when country was closing up, because there was no smoke, and smoke shows that all is well. If the proper managers can't burn or delegate, others might still try to, even at the wrong time – leaving country dirty only makes it dirtier and more fire-prone. 'You gotta burn, you don't burn then country will get poor, it will shut itself up ... no good for anybody then', and 'If everything is clean, the [D]reaming will be quiet.'[38]

People feel joy at well-burnt country. Fire 'brings the land alive again', central Arnhem Land elder Dean Yibarbuk declared, 'When we do burning the whole land comes alive again – it is reborn.'[39] Ida Ninganga recalled sadly, 'Oh, all of the islands, they would once be burning, from north, south and east and west, they would be burning, the smoke would be rising upwards for days, oh it was good ... you knew where all the families were, it was really good, in the times when the old people were alive', and Dinah Marrngawi exclaimed, 'Look! All of you, look to the distance, look north, look east, look west, the islands are burning, this is how it should be, this is how it was when the old people were alive, look this country is burning it has been lifted up, we have embraced it again.'[40]

The people of 1788 showed that making fire an ally works, that you can end killer fires or nearly, that fire is key to protecting species diversity and abundance, that land can be made beautiful. Taming fire was a great achievement. But the Australia this made – grass on good soil, forest split by grass, undergrowth uncommon – exactly suited invading stockmen. Land for kangaroos was also ideal for stock. Making grass paved the way for the pastoral prosperity of Australia. It put Australia on the sheep's back. This cruelly and tragically dislodged generations of knowledge, lifetimes of skill and care, and left the land open to ignorance and plunder.

1788 FIRE NOTES

1. Know your country
Fire acts on local conditions which can change even over short distances, so it's important to know the local terrain, its soil and soil cover, and each species of plant and animal, bird, reptile and insect (hereafter animal) in it. Know where each lives, how specialised its habitat is, if it migrates, when it flowers or breeds, and how it responds to fire – how easily it can avoid or escape, how well it recovers afterwards. Since plants and animals differ in their life and breeding cycles, know where core country is for each, which have alternative habitats, and so on.

In 1788 this immense task was addressed in two linked ways: a family learnt and taught its own ground, and people learnt and taught their totem and its habitat. Two specialist knowledges thus interacted to ensure safe fire and ecological wellbeing, allowing expert burning over both small family patches and extensive landscapes.

2. Know your weather
Learn especially to predict rain and wind by watching clouds, feeling changes in humidity and air pressure, and watching animal behaviour. Learn when dew falls – usually two or three dewy nights signal that more will follow. Learn how wind slackens, and how fire can generate its own wind.

3. Know why you are burning
On the same country, why you burn might vary from year to year. For example grass, yams and orchids can all share country, but their fire timing differs. To harvest yams you burn to expose them when they are ripe in early summer, which is before most seed grasses head. To harvest seed you burn in autumn after the seed has ripened. To promote orchid bulbs you burn a slightly hotter fire, usually in summer, and harvest the next year. Sometimes people might not hunt or harvest at all, to build up resources to host a ceremony.

4. Know what area you are burning
Know where to start a fire, at what time of day, where its flanks will run, and when and where it will go out. 'You sing the country before you burn it,' Dean Yibarbuk says. 'In your mind you see the fire, you know where it is going, and you know where it will stop. Only then do you light the fire.'

5. Discuss with neighbours
The bigger the fire the more neighbours to consult. For big fires, fire experts, from whichever group they come, would be called in to guide or adjudicate. More distant communities will know by the smoke whether country is being properly burnt.

6. Backburn vulnerable places

For ecological or cultural reasons, some places should not be burnt or should be burnt differently from a main fire. Preliminary backburning protects fire-sensitive plants, ceremony sites, conservation reserves, camps and water frontages. These are usually burnt early, when ground and plants are still damp, with small, precise fires, sometimes repeated over several days to treat a place properly. Beings might blind people who let fire into vulnerable or special places.

7. Choose the day

Local initiative is crucial. Locally, people know when a time to burn is approaching: the season plus the brittleness of the grass, for example, tells them. Even so, on the day of a burn elders and fire managers check wind and temperature before starting a fire, and perform appropriate ceremonies to make sure a fire succeeds.

8. Normally, use cool fire

See the 'Management Fires' table (pp. 108–9).

Occasionally hot fire is necessary, for example to kill off melaleuca scrub or push back wet forest or clean up country, but a lifetime might pass without such a fire being lit.

Cool fires are much easier to control. They trickle over the ground, make only white smoke, don't throw embers or damage tree canopies, give animals time to escape, leave bigger unburnt patches, don't germinate scrub, don't bake the soil or its creatures, and leave some litter unburnt and less ground bare.

Except perhaps in spinifex country, people would not usually burn at night. Fires burn differently then, under the influence of wind changes and sometimes increased humidity, and night fires are harder to patrol. A fire would usually go out or be put out about dusk and lit again the next day.

Almost all today's 'controlled' fires are for fuel reduction. Fuel has built up so much since 1788 that in many places cool fires are not possible, and traditional owners accept that fuel reduction will be necessary before a cool-fire regime can begin. Nonetheless the principles of cool fire apply to fuel reduction fires.

9. Burn in mosaics
Most fires and all cool fires make a mosaic of burnt and unburnt patches. Burnt patches are opportunities for plant regeneration, animal feeding, and hunting. Unburnt patches are refuges from which plants and animals can recolonise burnt ground. Skilful burning can locate burnt and unburnt patches quite precisely.

10. Burn to break up or slow down a fire
Examples are burning into the wind, burning into obstacles such as water, rock, cliffs or burnt ground, burning downhill, burning when plants and ground are damp or wet, and directing the flame front by choking its flanks.

To burn into the wind, ideally choose a light wind from the right quarter. No wind is OK, but it can let a fire create its own wind, hard to control. A light wind slows the fire front and is more likely to throw embers back onto burnt ground. Grass tends to bend downhill, so burning downhill is more likely to stop a fire cresting along the stalks.

In 1788 people could fight hot fires if they had to, usually by backburning. When a bushfire menaced an eastern Riverina homestead in the 1870s, and the stockmen were away, an elder organised women and boys to run a chessboard of spot fires across the approaching front.[1] The burnt patches broke up the fire and it was easily put out.

11. Start now
Apart from an invaluable scatter of Aboriginal fire experts, almost no one today has the knowledge to use 1788 fire for fuel control and species protection. We must learn to burn and burn to learn. Climate change will make this harder. This is no argument against 1788 fire: climate change is making every fire control method harder. The quicker we start on 1788 fire the better.

8

BABES IN THE WOOD

HERITAGE UNSEEN

On 28 April 1770 Joseph Banks saw at Botany Bay 'trees ... not very large and stood separate from each other without the least under wood'. On 1 May James Cook walked on Botany Bay land 'diversified with woods, lawns and marshes; the woods are free from underwood of every kind and the trees are at such a distance from one another that the whole country or at least a great part of it might be cultivated without being obliged to cut down a single tree'.[1] Both men found this plant distribution noteworthy. Neither asked why it was so. They came from England via the tropics, places where such landscapes were unheard of, unless they were made.

They were made, but Cook and Banks had the newcomer habit of not seeing this, let alone of wondering why. Newcomers thought the land natural. They assumed that primitive hunter-gatherers lacked the skill and inclination to make country. Yet they commonly used a word that meant exactly that: 'park'. Parks were how Europe's gentry made land, deliberately associating water, grass and trees in picturesque array. In Australia newcomers saw parks but not gentry. Robert Dawson thought the country inland from Port Stephens (NSW)

> truly beautiful: it was thinly studded with single trees, as if planted for ornament ... It is impossible therefore to pass through such a country ... without being perpetually reminded of a gentleman's park and grounds ... The first idea is that of an inhabited and improved country, combined with the pleasurable associations of a civilized society.[2]

Hundreds of such remarks came from every part of Australia, even the far inland, that harsh country that horrified and sometimes killed newcomers.[3]

Fire and no fire made parks, yet newcomers tried to stop people burning. In March 1839, just over two years after South Australia was founded, judge Henry Jickling warned a jury,

> A native, named Williamy, is accused of wilfully and maliciously setting fire to the grass. It is quite certain that [this] ... must be put a stop to ... [but was the prisoner acting] 'wilfully and

maliciously'... it is common, and, in the estimation of most savage tribes, a necessary and laudable practice annually to burn off the withered grass on their hunting grounds to facilitate and hasten the growth of the young grass of which the native animals are so fond ... It is possible, therefore, that the native prisoner may have imagined that he was only doing what he and his tribe have always been accustomed to do ... we should warn the natives of the dangers which they incur by the practice ... before we can inflict a proportionate punishment.[4]

Tairmunda (Williamy) may have been lucky. At Port Lincoln (SA) in December 1854, at least three men were charged with setting fire to grass and one spent a fortnight in prison for it, and in April 1856 four district men got two months in prison for the same offence.[5] In 1847 Western Australia sanctioned the flogging of any Aboriginal person who lit a fire between September and March,[6] though some newcomers opposed such cruelty. Francis Singleton, a resident magistrate south of Perth, advised,

The herbage, unless it has been burnt in the previous summer becomes exceedingly hard, and is usually refused by the stock ... To frame a statute forbidding the Natives to fire the bush would I fancy prove abortive; and could such a law be carried out in practice I should conceive it to be an unjust one. The Aborigines look forward to the summer season with the same feelings as Europeans. To both it is the time of harvest. It is then they gather in by means of these fires their great harvests of game,[7]

but within a year a flogging ordinance was passed. North-west of Belyando (Qld) in September 1880, a young girl was mortally wounded when her family were 'dispersed' after a fire got away while they were fishing 'on the territory of the tribe'.[8] Today people still risk prosecution to burn country.[9]

TOO LITTLE FIRE

Each winter after a big fire, television shows locals joyful at the bush regenerating, while photographers make exhibitions from green shoots on black trunks. Better to see this as fuel building up, to end in another killer fire twenty to forty years on. In 1788 people would never have let that happen. Big fires were rare, but after one, people cool-burnt patches of new growth, some big, some small, some as habitats, some as refuges, then over the years kept these plains and clearings open as the bush grew around. It was no accident that newcomers delighting in 1788's parks so often reported no 'underwood'. That not only made parks; it was a vital fuel control.

'No fire' is normal among newcomers. As a result, the land quickly degraded. As early as the 1810s John Macarthur's land near Sydney 'had become crowded – choked up in many places by thickets of saplings and large thorn bushes (*Bursaria spinosa*) [Christmas bush, blackthorn] and the sweet natural herbage had for the most part been replaced by coarse wiry grasses which grew uncropped'.[10] Thomas Mitchell lamented,

> The omission of the annual periodical burning by the natives, of the grass and young saplings, has already produced in the open forest lands nearest to Sydney, thick forests of young trees, where, formerly, a man might gallop without impediment, and see whole miles before him. Kangaroos are no longer to be seen there; the grass is choked by underwood ... These consequences, although so little considered by the intruders, must be obvious to the natives.[11]

Beyond the Blue Mountains a mere two decades of grazing and fire suppression let unpalatable fire-sensitive plants like cassia, budda and yarran smother 1788 grass,[12] and where white cypress grew in 1788 as open woodland and people could 'see for miles', it steadily thickened until it was a weed impossible to force through.[13] West of the Dawson (Qld) in 1844, Ludwig Leichhardt saw open eucalypt forest and grass recently burnt; by 1917 that forest was 'thickly timbered, with much undergrowth'.[14] Eric Rolls convincingly demonstrated the same thing in the Pilliga (NSW) forest, and remarked, 'Australia's dense forests are not the remnants of two hundred years of energetic clearing, they are the product of one hundred years of energetic growth.' He noted that Henry Dangar's 'open grass land' south of the Manning (NSW) in February 1826 had become 'a wooded tangle' a century later.[15] Australia is dotted with names of places once open, now forest – Bald Hill, Bare Hill, Grassy Hill, One Tree Hill, Kangaroo Ground. A newcomer habit of converting such parks to wilderness by not burning continues today, so scrub and rainforest spread, forest fills in, choice perennials give way to less edible grasses.

To stop this, some early graziers saw the value of cool fire and tried to imitate it, but they too might be prosecuted for burning, and they lacked the precision to burn properly. In southwest Australia HW Bunbury wrote in 1836,

> [By the] extensive bush fires ... every two or three years ..., the country is kept comparatively free from under wood and other obstructions, having the character of an open forest through most parts of which one can ride freely; otherwise, in all probability, it would soon become impenetrably thick ... This has already been proved in the case of Van Diemen's Land, where, in consequence of the transportation of the Natives to Great or Flinders Island, and the consequent absence of extensive periodical fires, the bush has grown up thick to a most inconvenient degree ... It is true that we might ourselves burn the bush, but we could never do it with the same judgement and good effect as the Natives, who keep the fire within due bounds, only burning those parts they wish when the scrub becomes too thick or when they have any other object to gain by it,[16]

and a western Victoria pioneer observed, 'all the country around here ... was covered with kangaroo grass – splendid summer feed for stock of all kinds ... The country was like this for some years after 1846, until destroyed by the indiscreet use of fire.'[17] In the south by the 1940s perennials like kangaroo grass were mostly refugees in reserves where stock and improvers couldn't get at them.

On the West Australian south coast grazier Lew Scott recalled of the 1920s,

> native grass in those days, you don't see it now ... Because it's not burnt, you have to burn to get native grass ... you would light it up at about ten o'clock in the morning and three or four o'clock it would all go out, the next day you would light it up again. The bush was alive with possums and wallabies and kangaroo rats. The fire only went slowly ... it was only a little fire, it never used to get up in the trees and burn the possums ... the real oldies followed the burning patterns of the natives in keeping the place green ... learnt to burn little patches, that they wanted for their existence the same as the blackfellow – of course not winter and not spring – because you kill all the little birds and animals – and so summer burning.[18]

Try summer burning now!

WRONG FIRE

A Darling River pioneer noted 'a remarkable characteristic of the aborigine ... the care taken by them to prevent bushfires. In my long experience I have never known any serious bushfire caused by the blacks'.[19] After 1788 bushfire went wild. Uluru elders explained,

> After Pirampa (white people) arrived Anungu were forced to move away or were discouraged from looking after country the

old way, by patch burning. That was when Anungu first started to see the huge bushfires that have killed off the country, in summers after years of good rainfall. When the first Pirampa started burning, Anungu were very worried because white people did not know the proper way to burn, nor did they know where the sacred places were, and so they burnt places that should have been left alone.[20]

When JC Rogers arrived in Gippsland in 1902, old hands told him of

the open, clean-bottomed, park-like state of the forests ... it had been the accepted thing to burn the bush, to provide a new growth of shorter sweet feed for the cattle ... The practice was to burn the country as often as possible, which would be every three or four years according to conditions. One went burning in the hottest and driest weather in January and February, so that the fire would be as fierce as possible, and thus make a clean burn ... [This] resulted in a great increase of scrub in all timbered areas except the box country. The fires forced the trees and scrub to seed and coppice, and in time an almost impenetrable forest arose.[21]

In the north, similarly changing fire from cool to hot caused a 'widespread crash' of fire-sensitive blue cypress populations.[22] Which fire to use varied locally and seasonally, but cool fire was normal.

PREVENTION

How could people in 1788 possibly have survived today's killer fires? They could never outrun them, and the chances of rain arriving time after time to save them were nil. How could they survive the aftermath, the black lands where a day's fire might eat a year's food? How could they outlive the shame of such devastation? Killer fires must have decimated each generation in turn, and fire would have been a horror to Aboriginal people.

It was not. Since people could not outrun black days, they prevented them. If ever a people lived by the proverb 'Prevention is better than cure', it was the people of 1788. Instead of today's 'Prevent bushfires', the rough rule was 'A fire a day keeps bushfires away'. People planned fires yet allowed for fire caused by lightning, escape burns and war. Without such provision land management was at best a risk and at worst pointless. Planned burning meant that in most places there was simply not enough fuel for killer fires, and where there was, for example in dense forest with scrub, people ringed it with open country heavily grazed or frequently burnt. I once guessed that they kept out of such places at dangerous times, but summer, the peak fire-danger season, is precisely when people visited high country forests.

Reportedly the south-east's most dangerous fires are in these forests, typically dominated by mountain ash or alpine ash. Experts say that fires there can't be controlled. This is alarmingly close to saying that because newcomers can't control fire there, people in 1788 couldn't. In any case it's wrong. Mountain ash withstands moderate fire – that's why tree butts are so often fire-blackened. In June 2013 Neil Barraclough of East Gippsland emailed me:

> Just started reading *The Biggest Estate on Earth*, well done. So far I only disagree with your blanket statement that Mountain Ash *E. regnans* was burnt infrequently in very hot fires. The early fallers told me that many of the pre-European stands they logged were often of mixed age when ring counted back to pre-European times. This indicates to me that the stands were regularly burnt and this kept the fuel loads down so the fires didn't get hot enough to kill the mature trees. The early bushmen I spoke to supported this ...

Fire-made clearings and plains speckle the mountain country, though closing in now. Mountain cattlemen still use them, and Tom Griffiths notes them and summarises evidence of widespread Aboriginal occupation of mountain ash country – seasonally, he thinks,[23] but that's so everywhere. After Victoria's 1939 fires, Commissioner Leonard Stretton reported that early Gippsland settlers 'found for the greater part a clean forest ... open and traversible by men, beasts and wagons ... to-day in places where our forefathers rode, driving their herds and flocks before them, the wombat and the wallaby are hard put to it to find a passage'. He concluded that fire should be prevented more than fought.[24]

Since the people of 1788 could open such dangerous country with fire, why can't we now? To let bush go wild after a fire sets up the next fire. Why wait for that? Black land offers a chance to break the fire cycle. As soon as it shows a green tinge, we should start patch-burning, speckling clearings and refuges through the bush.

That implies an Australia-wide network of local fire prevention programs. Not firefighting plans – we have those. Prevention programs would emphasise local experts, firefighter and Aboriginal. They would accumulate expertise, burning cautiously at first, learning the district's plants and animals, steadily shifting resources from fighting to prevention and species protection, making sure the next fire finds less fuel. Properly resourced and supported, such a network could rescue us with far fewer resources than we now use firefighting, or more exactly fire failing. Somewhere will burn every summer. The question is, who decides when and how much – us, or nature?

FUEL REDUCTION

In 1788 controlling fuel did not mean fuel reduction fires. Planned fire made them superfluous. Fuel was a resource. It was rationed, not eliminated. There was plenty of tall grass around Cook's Endeavour River camp when Guugu Yimithirr men set it alight on 19 July 1770.[25] People used fuel to choose, to plan, to distribute. Clean-up fires reduced fuel, but as part of a planned fire cycle, not as an end in themselves. Until say the 1950s most newcomer fire too was done by landholders not to reduce fuel, but to promote green pick. The move in emphasis from private to government fire shifted focus from grass to trees and scrub, and from frequent to infrequent burning.

Naturally fuel built up, and in the 1920s officials began talking of a fire so new that we still don't have an agreed name for it – fuel reduction, hazard reduction, prescribed burning, protective burning, control burning, fuel control – names collectively declaring national dislocation in facing fire. In 1939 Commissioner Stretton found that 'Controlled Burning' should be official policy, though not in mountain ash country.[26] He was largely ignored, and his 1944 report on the Yallourn district fires was obliged to repeat,

> Not nearly enough protective burning is carried on ... The effectiveness of this form of defence is made manifest by the fact that parts of the forest which had been burned within the last year or so ... were unscathed. They are now standing as green oases in a wilderness of destruction.[27]

Today many foresters and firefighters argue that 'prescribed burning, done properly, is highly effective at mitigating the bushfire threat, even under severe weather conditions', and that 'Extreme Bushfires are not "natural disasters", as the government claims. They are undoubtedly caused by government's negligence towards hazard-reduction.'[28] Newcomers have steadily brought fuel reduction fire into prominence until it is now common, around the world ironically identifying Australians as fire specialists.

After its scarifying experience in the 1961 fires that burnt 1.8 million hectares, Western Australia developed planned forest fuel reduction cycles. It has had few big fires since – 1978, 1995, 2003, 2015–16 – these last after the program was scaled back following public pressure over a perceived threat from cool fire to wildlife. In 1979 the Forests Department published *Forest Fire Behaviour Tables for Western Australia*, upgrading it in 1985 and 2011. It lists factors influencing fire intensity, including temperature, canopy cover, scrub height, litter depth and weight, soil and plant moisture, dew point, rainfall variance, wind and so on, and applies these variably to different forest types – karri, northern jarrah, southern jarrah, wandoo, several pines etc. The result is so detailed that by the time you read it all the west could have been burnt out, but you don't have to read it all, just what applies to your local area – before fire comes. Its focus is on fuel reduction and it burns bigger blocks than in 1788, but its species protection benefits are obvious. It is the best Western-style fire control plan for forest country in Australia. Black Summer's 2019–20 fires burnt out 24 million hectares in the eastern states, but only 26,000 hectares in the south-west.[29] That's still too much, and in 2020–21 there were smaller but very damaging fires north-east of Perth, mostly on private land barely touched by fuel reduction, but the west offers newcomers a chance to learn to burn.

In most places modern control burning is centralised, costly, cumbersome, erratic, suspected and inadequate. It waits for the 'right' conditions – not summer usually (1788's peak fire season), a cool day, little wind, weeks of bureaucracy, an anxious watch on the result. It might abandon a proposed burn because the paperwork hasn't come through or because when it does the conditions are no longer right. Control seems the priority, but not fuel control. This is built-in failure. Mick Holton, president of the Volunteer Fire Fighters Association (NSW), argues,

> One of the biggest hindrances to hazard reduction is the 29-page, Bushfire Environmental Assessment Code. If fire managers carry out hazard reductions that contravene the code, they can be prosecuted ... Local fire brigades used to manage their own fire risk, and this proved a lot more successful. The focus was on local brigades performing low intensity burns in the off season. All planning and execution were done at the local level ... without the red tape[. This] offered superior environmental outcomes, enhanced protection of the community ... and a safer working environment for the fire fighters.[30]

Red tape means red fire.

2021 has fire problems unknown in 1788. Climate change makes fire prevention harder and more dangerous, but this is cause to start prevention programs, not stop them. 2021 also has 'assets': buildings, fences, crops and so on. Yet in 1788 people had special places they backburnt to protect – why can't we do more of that? Flammable exotic plants also add to today's fire challenges. Buffel grass, introduced over a century ago and spreading in the Centre, burns fiercely, wafting tiny seeds far on fire winds. But people are learning to manage it. Near Ernabella (SA) in 2014, three senior women burnt buffel grass tussocks for months, watching to learn when and how to control it. One, Tjariya, remarked, 'He's a mean one that one, but we'll beat him.'[31]

There is not enough fuel reduction, in two ways. First, it's commonly done when it's easiest, which is often the wrong time. A Sydney comparison found that most 1788–1845 fires were in spring to early summer, but 60 per cent of 1990s prescribed fires were in autumn to winter.[32] Second, it can be token. About 2016 Victoria shifted its burn targets from a benchmark system to the minister's discretion, and lobbying has made ministers very discreet. Compared with Western Australia's 6 per cent,[33] Victoria and New South Wales burn less than 1.5 per cent annually, so about 85 per cent of bushland carries fuel older than ten years.[34] Worse, what is burnt gives little thought for any creature in the way, let alone for all of them. Primitive. If 1788 fire is the university of land care, control burning is the creche.

Fuel reduction treats fire as untrustworthy. On our fire-prone continent this is a mistake, for it accepts landscapes out of control as normal. Nonetheless it will remain our most common fire type for many decades, because the land is indeed out of control, and because fuel reduction is the only fire we even half-comprehend. Even traditional owners say that this fire is needed for years to come, until the country is sufficiently set up to start 1788 fire. We must learn to reduce fuel before we can hope to begin more sophisticated fire management and use it to protect species.

SPECIES PROTECTION

Here are eight steps from fuel reduction to estate management:
1. The more fuel is reduced, the more easily is fire controlled, so the more useful it is.
2. Even hot fires leave unburnt patches, but the cooler the fire the bigger the patches.
3. Patch size can be adjusted by varying fire intensity.

4. Intensity can be regulated by fire frequency and fire timing (day, season, year).
5. Frequency and timing are local. They depend on local flora and local moderators like rain, wind, temperature and aspect.
6. The better people understand these variables, the more they can burn with purpose. They can move from limiting fuel to shaping country.
7. This lets them selectively locate fire-tolerant and fire-sensitive plants and arrange them conveniently and predictably, so that one resource supplies what another does not.
8. This gives plants the best possible growing conditions and animals a welcoming habitat, putting the best feed (burnt patches) next to the best shelter (unburnt country).

1788 fire thus moved far beyond fuel reduction. It put every species, every totem, in a habitat each not merely tolerated, but preferred. Today this skill could help answer key questions about endangered species. Why did they flourish then? How was their habitat conserved? What changes have damaged it since? Think how many plants and animals have declined or become extinct since 1788. No network of totem specialists alert to changes in range or abundance or habitat guarded them. Often we didn't even notice their going until too late or nearly, nor even now do we know why some vanished. To learn, to save, we must understand what Australia was like in 1788 (see Chapter 5).

For decades koalas, for example, have been reduced by diseases like chlamydia and by logging and land clearing. Governments have tried to balance, though hardly even-handedly, how many hectares koalas need against how many hectares loggers and farmers want. Such calculations ignore fire. Fire is not built into our land management thinking. Move only a little from control burning and fire disappears. As a result, Black Summer killed half the koalas in New South Wales and over 70 per cent in northern New South Wales.[35] On Kangaroo Island (SA) 80 per cent of koalas died.[36] Hardly a koala habitat anywhere was unaffected: after the flames they had nowhere to go. No planner allowed for this. Then in 2020 platypus were put on the endangered list. Around the world these animals speak at once of Australia. Now they face extinction. If we can't protect even them, what hope do other species have?

Protecting species takes skill. Universal principles on maintaining habitats and resources must be applied via detailed knowledge of local plants and animals: where they are, how they behave, when their young are vulnerable, whether they welcome or tolerate or dislike fire. Only locally is it possible to know when, where, how much and how often to burn. Even that may not be enough. After finding about 100 living Wollemi pines, the 'dinosaur trees' until 1994 best known as 90-million-year-old fossils, researchers spent years laboriously translocating seedlings. By 2019 they had translocated 400 pines. In one location only four of 218 survived Black Summer.[37] Its habitat presumably fire-free for 90 million years, we undid that in less than twenty-five.

In 1788 fire involved everyone, some more, some less, but all treated it with respect and freed it knowing beforehand how it would behave. Plans were made, ceremonies done, the interests of species respected, even little children instructed on what and when to burn, and seasonal fire programs negotiated – small within the family, big with neighbours and experts.

In whitefella fire, controlled or not, species must take their chance. Farms I worked on in the 60s always had a truck or trailer standing by in summer, water tank full, pump tested every morning. In the paddocks eyes scanned for smoke, and if seen a hasty call to the party-line switch located it, and anyone near enough raced to fight it. For generations white Australians fought fires that way, with branches or a flap of rubber or wet hessian nailed to a stick, with backpacks and backburning, with days of hard work if necessary, the women making cups of tea and cake. Only once do I recall thinking of species protection: when we harrowed around a dam where brolgas danced. No brolgas dance there now.

Species protection adds immense complexity to any fire plan. Today this complexity splits firies from greenies, often hostile to each other. This badly misses the big picture. It blocks a crucial alliance of great potential. Since habitat and species protection depend on fuel reduction, and since fuel reduction is pivotal to saving lives and property, fuel reduction programs should bring firies and greenies together. Our lengthening fire seasons are great persuaders in converting people to the need to make fire a friend. In this we're beginners, children. We import planes and firefighting teams, we ask thousands of volunteers to risk their lives, but we can't stop big fires. They burn for weeks or months. Officials declare fire categories like Emergency, Watch and Act, and Advice, but none mean a fire is out or even under control – all simply advise how soon people should get out. Not one of Black Summer's big fires was put out by firefighters. Not one. Instead we prayed for rain. When other societies do that, we think them superstitious savages. No wonder our main effort for species in a big fire is to count the losses afterwards.

We will fight big fires for decades to come. We should refine our firefighting, finding ways to reduce big fires, otherwise our only refuges in the bush might become land already burnt. We should accept the great gift 1788 offers, and progressively shift the weight of our fire efforts from fighting to prevention. We will never go back to 1788, but we could learn much from it, and make a country that protects all its creatures – even one day a country the old people might approve of.

9

POOR FELLA MY COUNTRY

RED RAMPAGE

Francis MacCabe's *Plan of the Survey of the Genoa River, Part 2, 1847*,[1] maps the dominant vegetation around Mallacoota Inlet (Vic) up to its head, naming a mosaic of plant communities, mostly 'open forest' (see pp. 48–51). For a surveyor in 1847, 'open forest' meant trees enough apart to drive a horse and cart through, so no scrub, the deadly fire layer. But it isn't all open forest. The coast north is 'lightly timbered', then 'well grassed open forest', then moving inland 'good herbage', then 'thickly timbered', then 'open forest'. How could such variety be?

The people of 1788 made that mosaic with fire. In places the plan shows you why. Where there is fresh water there is also grass, notably above the tidal reach. Before 1847 squatters took that country, south on 'good undulating open forest country having some ridges well grassed', north on 'gently undulating forest country ... some good grass'. Thick timber was there because some plants and animals prefer it, but open forest boxes it in. Not only do the lighter fuel loads circling the timber make it more fire-safe, but people knew where forest resources were and could harvest them predictably.

Not far away, in November 2014 John Mulligan showed me kilometres of thick bush from Cann River towards Mallacoota that was grass when he was a boy, and pointed out places where the Country Fire Authority (CFA) had let catastrophic fuel levels build up. John said that the CFA would burn a roadside strip and count the whole block as control burnt, and did too little even of that. Born in 1931, he was seriously alarmed at how dense and dangerous the bush had become in his lifetime.

When Victoria's Forestry Commission was established in 1919, John wrote, it imported a no-fire policy, believing that fire 'damaged the timber'. In West Gippsland and in the north it enforced this policy, but could not restrain the habitual burning of East Gippsland landholders. There constant fire kept the bush so open that you could canter a horse through it, cattle stayed in it on good feed year-round, and smoke was 'something we learned to live with'. 'So fuel built up in the West but not in the East.' In January 1939 much of West Gippsland and the north was burnt out, while although it had many small fires, East Gippsland was not. But from about 1950 the Forestry Commission was increasingly able to enforce its 'minimum burn practices'. This let fuel build across Gippsland, resulting in the big 1983 fires and many smaller but still serious fires.[2] By 2014 John was certain another big fire was festering.

In September 2016 the Mallacoota Safety & Resilience Committee held a fire-safety field day. In many places the only road into the village was lined with dense forest filled in with thick scrub reaching beyond sight. Fuel lay waiting. No one could outrun a big fire there, in 1788 or in 2016: it was a fire trap.

Many Mallacoota people knew the danger. Some said they'd go to the beach if fire came, but others thought that this seriously, perhaps fatally, misjudged what might happen. John warned that fuel reduction burning had been 'completely inadequate, with the result that we are now sitting on the biggest time bomb that East Gippsland has faced, because of the massive fuel loads'. Forester Vic Jurskis, also at the field day, similarly warned in January 2019, 'If we get fires under the same weather conditions today [as in 1939], they'll destroy everything from Bairnsdale to Sydney.'[3]

We know what happened. An unstoppable firestorm. A quarter of Mallacoota burnt. Refugees on the beach, as they said they would be, who had to be rescued by sea. Blankets of white ash, meaning fire over 1000 degrees. Flames jumping crests just as in 1939. 172 years after MacCabe's plan showed us 1788 Australia, it came to this. Shameful.

Fires need fuel. Big fires need a lot of fuel. What people did at Mallacoota until newcomers began stopping them reduced and dispersed fuel, breaking it up with grazed grass and open forest. That changed almost everywhere in Australia after 1788. Huge tracts now carry much more fuel than they did, letting fires run, unstoppable, for hundreds of kilometres. It didn't need anything particularly special to spark Black Summer's 2019–20 fires, just drought, hot winds, and fuel. Sooner or later, climate change or not, the bush burns. Our task is to reduce fuel while maintaining the beauty and diversity of our plants and animals.

Like the Dreaming, like Songlines, Black Summer showed us past, present and future. We saw the consequence of our neglect, the devastation that caused, and a warning for the years ahead. We saw immense human effort, courage, mateship, skill, wondrous firefighting equipment and technology, strong community support, an international rally of resources, and huge expense. The result? The worst fires we've ever had. We're getting nowhere. Not every summer will be as terrible as 2019–20, but big fires come faster and faster upon us. This is our country to care for, but we can't do it. We live with a national disgrace.

Fire has always been part of being Australian, but what that means has been upended since 1788. Then it meant maintaining an alliance; now it means fighting an enemy. Or, to judge from some responses to Black Summer, dodging an enemy. The prime minister claims, 'We have had bushfires before and will have them again, nothing to see here, this is all part of a normal cycle',[4] then for the cameras obliges stricken survivors to shake his hand. A scientist declares control burns 'not the answer' yet adds that they have not been properly tested, even though Black Summer delivered the biggest field trial in our history. Others have the gall to say publicly that control burning costs too much. What price Black Summer?

Experts, including senior fire professionals, told the 2020 royal commission that control burning is not safe or useful. One said, 'The weight of research into the effects of fuel reduction on the propagation of extreme bushfires, indicates that as conditions deteriorate, fuel reduction is of diminishing effectiveness, and may have no appreciable effect under extreme conditions.'[5] You could step over a 1788 grass fire: what is the point of confining remarks to 'extreme conditions' when fuel reduction intends to ensure that there are none? What research prompted these bumbling and pointless remarks? None from Aboriginal fire experts. None from the record of history. None from the 1939 royal commission which declared, 'It is long established by foresters in other parts of the world that in [extreme] conditions ... [fuel reduction] is the only effective safeguard.'[6]

Climate change surfaced quickly as a culprit: 'a climate-change induced inferno ripped through NSW and Victoria'.[7] 'Climate-change induced'? No big fires before climate change became apparent? No 1851, 1898, 1926, 1939, 1944? All those killed people and burnt homes and hectares aplenty. It matters to know what 'induced' them.

Climate change is a real and urgent danger. Black Summer was south-east Australia's longest and harshest fire season. It generated an unimaginable twenty pyrocloud storms, when fire takes over the weather.[8] It killed fewer people but destroyed more homes, killed more wildlife, and in the south-east ruptured more Songlines and incinerated more sacred places than any before it. Yet to suggest that what happened 50, 100, 150 years ago was not enough to warn us of fire's danger ignorantly denies our fire history. We were warned. Our fault was not being caught by surprise, but not confronting what we knew was coming.

Big fire years are stepping stones in white Australia's history, each a lesson for the future. In Victoria on 6 February 1851, a suffocating day in a drought summer, hot northerlies linked up fires in remote bush that had been let burn for months. One started when bullock drivers left burning logs untended in the Plenty Ranges, and the wind took it racing away. From north-east to south-west a boomerang of fire took hold. The sky darkened, birds in flight dropped dead, thick smoke reached northern Tasmania, and a ship 20 miles (32 kilometres) off the Portland coast was drenched in burning embers. William Howitt reported, '300 miles in extent, and at least 150 [generally more like 50] in breadth, was reduced to a desert. It was one blackened and burning waste ... the country was actually one blaze for thousands of square miles.'[9] Twelve people died, over a million sheep, and uncounted thousands of cattle and wildlife.

This fire was only sixteen years after newcomers reached Victoria. It fed on crops and hay as well as forest and scrub, but its speed and extent so soon showed how readily the bush leaps into deadly flame. The next big fire, also in Victoria, was not until 1898, and for a century after 1851 all the big fires were in Victoria (1898, 1926, 1939, 1944, 1951–52). Extraordinary. Were newcomers in 1851 taught a lesson they remembered for fifty years, then forgot? If so, the lesson was not climate change, but fuel.

Significant elements of 1851 recurred in later big fires: a drought summer, remote fires let burn, a hot peak day (47 °C in 1851 vs 45 °C in 2019–20), hot northerlies, red flame leaping, distant places choked with smoke and showered with embers, spot fires, homes burnt, people killed. In January 1939 the fires

> leaped from mountain peak, to mountain peak, or far out into the lower country, lighting the forests 6 or 7 miles in advance of the main fires ... Houses of brick were seen and heard to leap into a roar of flame before the fires had reached them ... in many places, hundreds of trees of great size were blown clear of the earth, tons of soil, with embedded masses of rock, still adhering to the roots.[10]

That matches Black Summer intensity well before global warming was apparent.

But the 1851 and 1939 fires lasted a few days and peaked in one or two. 1851 burnt about five million hectares, about 22 per cent of Victoria; 1939 burnt uncounted 'millions of acres'. Terrible, but much less than the 1974–75 inland fires which burnt about 117 million hectares, or Black Summer which lasted six months and burnt over 24 million hectares, more than all Victoria. In the years between, the climate got hotter, and the fuel load got bigger. Today we don't hope to reverse global warming, only to limit or stabilise it by some future decade. We could start reducing fuel now.

AFTER BLACK SUMMER

Many Black Summer images of fire and black land show whipstick stands of youngish eucalypts. In southern Australia regrowth forest, burnt and not yet burnt, is common. If it were a plant category, as it usefully could be, it would be the most common category. Generations back that whipstick country was mostly grass or open forest. We let it run wild. Now we reap the whirlwind.

Notice something else. In 2019–20 and commonly earlier, the killer fires were all in southern Australia. There was no red rampage in the north or Centre. Perhaps there was no climate change across that vast region? Escape fires happen there, but almost all big fires are controlled. Neither results from not burning. In the south we focus on saving lives and houses after a fire takes hold; in the north and Centre they focus on prevention and control. They see ground to love and nurture with fire and no fire, which repays their ceremonies and care a thousandfold with comfort, abundance and beauty. This sustains every species, for all are equally entitled to the riches of the earth. People know well that this can never mean doing nothing. All things change, so all must be kept in balance – not only humans, but every plant, animal, bird, reptile and insect. Once it was like this in the south too.

In the south, rural fire brigades remain the fire front line, still mostly voluntary but increasingly professional. Men and women commit their lives to firefighting, while technology and command have been increased and centralised, on the face of it greatly expanding firefighting capacity – equipment, communications, planes. In 2021 we are better equipped, as distinct from better organised, than we have ever been.

Yet. As fire trends worsen while more equipment is assembled, local autonomy diminishes. Firefighting has become a state matter, and may become a national matter. As a result, fire management can't avoid focusing on fighting fires after they break out, sometimes days after. Key responses and equipment are centralised, so time lags let fires take hold and get worse.

The key to fire control is prevention (see Chapter 8). Here some local autonomy remains via control burns by brigades, farmers and volunteers, which in varying degrees state-based fire controllers approve or tolerate. Since we have let so much fuel build up, especially since the 1960s, this is sensible, though too many state-run burns are more for public relations than for fuel reduction. We would do better at fuel reduction by freeing local initiative.

We can't hope simply to chain fire up. We've tried that: it doesn't work. Learning to reduce fuel must take us further, teaching us to understand fire, to work with it, to see it as much a friend on the ground as in the fireplace. Perhaps not a friend – that might be asking too much of whitefellas – but at least an ally, a tool pivotal to helping all Australia's plants and creatures flourish, including us.

MINDSETS

Even that may be beyond us. The most calamitous impact on Aboriginal society took shape millennia before any white man saw Australia. In the Northern Hemisphere people became farmers.

Farmers think differently. Like their draught horses they wear the blinkers agriculture imposes. Farming means staying put, settling down, drawing lines on maps, building fences. Fences on the ground make fences in the mind.[11] Australia had not a single fence in 1788, not a single visible marker that cultivators might recognise as bounding property or claiming ownership. Management was practically invisible to the invaders. That let them transform fire from friend to fiend, judge its allies ignorant, and make Australia an unmanaged land, a terra nullius.

Newcomers are still in that mental vice. That's one reason why after over two centuries of occupation we are mostly still newcomers. There is a great irony in terra nullius, or 'the mere occupation of a desert or uninhabited land', as the Colonial Office put it with unconscious irony in 1822.[12] To occupy the continent, newcomers need not have chosen this excuse. Where they didn't choose it around the world, where they met farmers, they still took what they wanted. They invoked it here because they had no use for people who didn't farm. In 1688 William Dampier remarked that north-west coast people were 'the miserablest People in the World ... they have no Houses, but lye in the open air without any covering ... the Earth affords them no Food at all. There is neither Herb, Root, Pulse, nor any sort of Grain, for them to eat, that we saw.'[13] He saw no farms, so he saw no food. 150 years later that blindness remained common. The *Sydney Herald* declared in 1838,

> this vast country was to them a common ... their ownership, their right, was nothing more than that of the Emu or Kangaroo. They

bestowed no labour upon the land and that – and that only – it is which gives a right of property to it. Where, we ask, is the man endowed with even a modicum of reasoning powers, who will assert that this great continent was ever intended by the Creator to remain an unproductive wilderness?[14]

There is the irony. Australia had no wilderness in 1788, no terra nullius. It has now. It is we who converted country we can't use to fuel bombs in scrub, forest, park and even desert.

Our ignorance is compounded by arrogance: we know little, but we think we know a lot. We think we know more than 'wandering savages'. We build far into the bush, one road out, and let forest and scrub thicken around us. We see stock killed and farms blackened and think that's a problem for farmers and insurers, not a display of national ignorance. We see unique species driven to extinction by feral animals and habitat loss without a glimmer of recognition of the grief that causes Aboriginal people. Newcomers once shot and poisoned Aboriginal people wholesale, put them in prison for lighting fires, and deported communities and children off country forever, yet we still expect them to think like us about land.

Captured children apart, people rarely became like us. They kept to the Law. The Law explained the purpose of life and the service of all creatures to eternity. Its fusion of philosophy and ecology generated an all-embracing certainty that land is the mother of life, that all things have a place, that change must yield to balance, that caring for country depends on proper ritual and constant work, that in this work fire is an essential ally. Day by day, newcomers made clear their calamitous ignorance of managing land properly. Why would anyone want to become like that?

The key fact about 1788 fire and no fire is that it worked. In Black Summer Australia seemed alight, but not everywhere. In recent decades fire has invaded every capital city except, significantly, Darwin, while the north and the Centre, the wettest and driest parts of Australia, have big fires, but almost all are controlled. What happened in the south in the 2019–20 summer, east and west, did not happen there. Recently a US journalist researching fire in Kakadu remarked to a traditional owner that people down south feared fire. The traditional owner couldn't believe it. Again and again he checked if he'd heard right, each time in puzzled disbelief. He couldn't accept that anyone might think fire a foe.[15]

We can't call ourselves Australian if we can't care for the land. We should at least try to understand how it worked before we laid Europe over it. I see five stages of 1788 fire:

1. Give plants and animals the fire they prefer
2. Maintain diversity
3. Balance species
4. Ensure abundance
5. Locate resources conveniently and predictably.

These worked together, shifting from one to another as circumstance required. Today we can't do any of them. We don't attempt stage 1. We admire the objectives of stages 2–4, but Australia is more a world leader in species extinction than at any time in the past.[16] Three billion living creatures killed in six months. More survivors than usual dying in wasteland. Species on the edge. Compare this with stage 5, something we can't imagine. We can't even reduce fuel successfully, the essential condition for the rest. How often in Black Summer did we hear, 'We can't stop this fire' or 'Leave now, we won't be able to help' or 'The town was saved by a wind change', or most damning, 'Pray for rain'?

WHAT TO DO?

Much has changed since 1788. Australia endures continuing invasions of feral people, animals and plants, and an ignorant and increasing population much less evenly distributed than in 1788, most with eyes fixed on the wider world. If being Australian means being able to look after our own place, we have far to go. But we can try.

1. Think of fire year-round. Fuel accumulates year-round; think that way. Don't stop when the fires stop. Use the first months after a fire to cool-burn patches big and small in regenerating scrub, breaking up forest. In time the patches become clearings and refuges for people and animals as the bush grows around (see Chapter 8).
2. Think what is possible with fire and no fire. Learn what good it can do. Listen to people on country. Listen to landholders with traditions of fire as refreshing the land. Newcomers use the language of war against fire: fight, battle, attack, fire front, brigades. Given recent catastrophes, that mental block will persist for decades, but look beyond, to how fire might shape country and protect species.

3. Learn to burn and burn to learn. Develop as much technology, machinery and know-how to prevent fire as to fight it. Learn better control burning by doing more of it, guided by Aboriginal experts and firefighters with on-ground experience. There will be painful errors since we know so little and face more challenges than in 1788: fuel build-up, ignorance, assets, few resources committed to prevention, flammable feral plants, climate change. How to deal with most of these depends on local conditions, but for example in fuel-rich places we might burn in light rain, inch by inch, patch by patch, returning again and again, thinning bush out. This would need more resources than we now use, but less than people used in 1788. We must make fire an ally. Keep in mind what happens if we don't. Control burning is not a choice between fire and no fire, but between little fires often and big fires too often.

   Firefighters are hampered by public and political opposition to control burning. People fear escapes and object to animals fleeing or dying, choking smoke, black ash, polluted water, dirty washing, the risk of asthma and so on. Yet all this happened during Black Summer's fires, much worse than any control burn. Of course we must make more smoke now than in 1788, because we've let fuel build up. It is a daunting task to return towards 1788's safer balance, but 1788 shows us the rewards if we do, and black summers the future if we don't.

4. Act locally. Resist centralised decision-making. Use local knowledge to plan prevention, to get the timing right, to seize

the day when fire comes. Develop a network of local prevention programs, and back them with state resources for equipment, communications, training and youth programs. Recognise that while local control methods vary according to climate, vegetation and terrain, universal principles operate. The 1939 royal commission 'found that although different kinds of country have problems of fire prevention and suppression which differ to some degree, one from the other, nevertheless the general principles ... are of almost universal application',[17] while the 2020 royal commission concluded, 'risk should be managed by the lowest level of government that is capable of managing it', and emphasised local knowledge as vital for managing natural disasters.[18]

5. Introduce cultural burning into control burns. 1788 fire could make parks; we make ruin. With the best will in the world it could easily take a century or more to learn to control-burn properly, but it would be criminal to leave unaddressed the damage fire does to lives and species until then. Value cultural expertise.

6. Ask Aboriginal experts to lead in tackling a most serious challenge: to reconcile more frequent fire with species protection. Most experts want to teach. It is a way to care for country they no longer control, a way to resuscitate the safety, diversity and beauty their ancestors made. Some newcomers say that Aboriginal people today don't know much. True, most know less than the old people, but more than us,

they still have Law, and generations will stay on Country, accumulating lifetimes of local knowledge. Where will your descendants be?

Do not commandeer traditional expertise. Cultural burning is intellectual property. We should yield leadership and initiative in it, pay for it, back it with resources, and support carbon projects arising from it. Too often traditional owners say they are not asked to plan or initiate cultural burns, only to do the slog in a program given them. Not good enough. Not smart.

Imagine Aboriginal men and women in senior environmental policy positions. Imagine a national network of ranger programs, and collaborations between cultural fire and rural fire brigades. Imagine more Aboriginal-led companies managing fire and land for pastoral stations and mining companies, leading in carbon farming, and rescuing from extinction their totem allies.[19] What an Australia that would be, and what an example to the world.

1788's achievement was truly impressive. To balance land and people so richly for so long across so great an area ranks among humanity's great achievements. No other world civilisation managed it. Almost all turned from 'hunter-gathering' to agriculture, thence in time to a bad end or an uncertain future, such as ours. The people of 1788 farmed, but never joined the agrarian world's race to a complex technology. Fire and no fire gave too many advantages. It let them, alone of all earth's peoples, dedicate an entire continent to sustaining rather than depleting resources, even in the harshest places ensuring continuity for uncounted generations. No legacy was so intricately woven, or so brutally undone.

Poor fella my country.

10

HOW WE MIGHT LOVE MOTHER EARTH MORE

Valuing the earth and the raw materials it provides for us is an essential part of conservative economics. What is smart about eliminating the resource? We need to be careful and pay the correct price for every product. We must insist that our world survives as long as the sun. To deny the beauty of the natural world and the wonderful society of humans to other generations is the epitome of selfishness.

Every product we use must be stamped with our determination that our great-grandchildren can enjoy them in the future. This means our care must be extended to soil, water, food and the products we have created from the resources of the earth. We must extend the life of products so that the resource can regenerate or, in the case of minerals, be expended very conservatively.

So much decent timber is wasted on building sites as renovations take place. De-nailing timber is a time-consuming job, so a lot of perfectly good wood is sent to landfill or burnt on site. Changing this practice is just a matter of us setting different priorities at government level. If we charge the full price for the use of our forest resources, as we do for our minerals, then suddenly employing workers to de-nail and prepare recycled timber becomes a viable option.

The majority of trees in commercial forests in East Gippsland and on the far south coast of New South Wales are silvertop ash (*Eucalyptus sieberi*). This tree grows straight and its first limbs are quite high off the ground, so it is perfect for harvesting. Most of the harvested trees are used for the pulp timber processed at the Eden woodchip mill in southern New South Wales. Woodchips, which we sell for the absolute bargain basement price of A$260 per tonne,[1] are an incredibly unsustainable use of our forests and the forestry industry is supported by a plethora of grants, allowances, free roads and export incentives that come from the public purse.[2] Without that support it would not be possible to sustain the industry.

If we reconsidered the whole operation and the infrastructure the public supplies to prop it up, might it be possible to use the trees for greater benefit to the nation? It is important that such a change is at least employment neutral. Despite what the timber barons have told small timber-town residents, the massive loss of employment in the forestry industry over the past fifty years has not been caused by left-wing parties and greenies, but by mechanisation. In the 1970s it was nothing to find at least fifteen people working a forestry coupe, but in March 2021 I saw two forestry operations on the south coast where each was being conducted by just one person using one truck, one massive harvester and one loader.

None of these suggestions is anti-capitalism, but our barons become so incensed at any impediment to their freedom and make such a noise about it that we lose sight of the obvious economic opportunities in conducting industries under different ground rules. We tax tobacco and alcohol to bring about social change and to provide resources for government policy, but when we ask the mining industry to acknowledge the advantages they enjoy from having access to the national estate, all hell breaks loose. We are being tested by these barons, who expend the weight of their wealth on influencing government policy, but we need to resist those influences in order to protect our democracy and our speaker's chair from occupation by a mob with nothing but bitterness to add to the public good. Altering national public policy is not a lapse into communism but a mature adjustment of an economic and social system for the good of all, the common wealth.

A momentum shift is occurring in Australia. Far-right conservatives might snort with derision, but Australians are calling for their children to be taught a history truer to the real state of the sovereign Aboriginal economy prior to the invasion and a true retelling of the history that followed it. This is now something the government can't ignore, should not want to ignore.

A tangible demonstration of this shift took place in March 2021 in the old Picture House in Brunswick Heads on the north coast of New South Wales. Artist Craig Ruddy and his partner Roberto Meza combined with a team of fellow citizens for an event to raffle prizes, including one of Craig's paintings, and to run an auction to raise money to supply harvesting and threshing machines and equipment so that Black Duck Foods can continue to employ local Yuin people in the production of traditional Aboriginal foods at Yumburra. There was palpable support for a different way of looking at history and a determined push to adopt more sustainable agricultural practices. The funds were raised mostly from modest people who hauled notes out of their bags and wallets. There were gifts from more well-off people, too, but the amount of money raised from bar staff and pensioners on mobile scooters was the most startling. That community is now raising money for the local Bundjalung people's own agriculture program.

A proportion of the fund is being dedicated to supporting students in local schools, some of whom have already worked for a few days at our farm. This work isn't for everyone, but for those who do enjoy it we will be able to guarantee support for them to stay in school and plan a pathway into agricultural science or horticulture or any other course that could support their work on the farm. Our aim is that they take what they learn at Yumburra to other Aboriginal communities so that agriculture employment and training can be fostered.

Another proportion of the money will go to the design and manufacture of a seed harvester (see Chapter 2). The purpose of the machine, which will be called Mandu II (Bandicoot), is to provide us with a wider harvester that is nevertheless sufficiently manoeuvrable to harvest in the 10–12 trees per acre forest we are moving towards. Diversity is maintained in this forest because we know that we can harvest up to five or six grasses in this way over two seasons. We can also harvest the tubers of orchids and lilies on this complex grassland.

If we can continue to control cats and foxes on our land, we will consolidate the return of bandicoots and dunnarts. I had never seen a dunnart until I was shifting a tangle of burnt logs after the recent fires. A dozen little creatures hopped out of the heap like miniature kangaroos, closely followed by a tiger snake. These beautiful animals are seed eaters and they came back because the grass came back. We removed the cattle three years ago and the grass was able to go to seed. We harvest around 80 per cent of the seed but there is more than enough left for the dunnarts and rejuvenation of the grassland.

Bandicoots have an important role in this ecosystem. They eat small fungi in the soil and by digging for it they make small cone-shaped divots that act as receptors for rainfall, thus preventing run-off. The divots also receive falling seed and act as nursery tubes. The bandicoots act as conduits for the spread of fungal matter, which forms important networks of communication and nutrition between plants. Bandicoots are known to churn tonnes of soil every year, gently mixing in plant material from the surface. They are mulch creators. If we understood their role in the extraordinary tilth of Australian soils, as witnessed by the first Europeans, we would be making every effort to allow them their previous honourable role in soil building.

THE GOD PRINCIPLE

It is impossible not to talk about how our society and economy are organised: they incorporate the foundation beliefs that directly impact our home, the earth. If the free market system, and communism for that matter, worked, and its excesses were not endangering our home, then the people of Africa would not starve periodically, COVID-19 vaccines would be distributed equitably, people would not be living broken lives on the streets of rich cities, there would be no threat to endangered species, and drug use would not be at such phenomenal levels.

In the past, humans were never in a position to destroy the earth. Now we are, and our folly is explained away as collateral damage of our system of society and economy. The earth is not our collateral, we are hers. We must demand that responsibility be taken for the things business and government do in our name. If we do not object and follow up with legislation and penalties, then we are just coughing into our hankies. As we have seen in earlier chapters of this book, some of the outcomes of this process of common wealth resource exploitation are the destruction of soil and groundwater, and uncontrolled fire. If we are serious about recovery from recent fires and protection from future fires, we may need to develop new social principles or go back to the six original Christian commandments (there are six commandments about morality and four about God's ego) and really assert the power of their inherent virtue, rather than pay mawkish lip service to their importance as comfortable platitudes at bedtime.

When Russians drained the Aral Sea to irrigate their cotton plantations,[3] the world tut-tutted but turned away because it was just a by-product of enterprise. It didn't matter that the communists were taking industrial agriculture to an illogical conclusion – the business principle was sacrosanct. Sacred business.

When the soils of America's Midwest blew away as a result of excessive ploughing and whole populations were impoverished, it was seen, once again, as the collateral damage of progress. We wrote a book about it, *The Grapes of Wrath*, and we taught it to our children. But nothing changed.

When we cleared all the trees from Victoria's light mallee soils, that soil blew away to swathe Melbourne and Port Phillip Bay in red dust. We said it was merely the cost of settling soldiers after World War II. No black soldiers were included, mind you, but we rightfully rewarded our damaged white men for fighting people in a different hemisphere.

When our miners blew up a cave of a people's sacred art 41,000 years older than most world art,[4] it was just an accident. When an ammonia plant was built at the throat of a gallery of a million carvings on the Burrup Peninsula near Karratha in the Pilbara region of Western Australia,[5] it was just a business decision. Not intimidation, not contempt, business! But the plant could have been built anywhere on that flat peninsula.

Our business is not separate from our religion. Capitalism and Christianity have evolved together. The principle of 'Love thy neighbour', established as central to the philosophy of the Christian empire, soon became selective. Self-interest and prejudice undermined the egalitarian foundation of the religion and the edifice began to crumble. The people's houses became castles and cloisters. We are responsible for both capitalism and Christianity. If the philosophy is threatening to destroy our planet we must change. It does not mean we swing from one extreme ideology to another: we go back to the six commandments of the Christian faith or the bedrock principles of Islam, those which talk about the sacredness of life and the search for peace and kindness.

It is not an edifying reflection of our philosophical rigour that both of these religions state that humans shall have dominion over the earth as if we are God's chosen ones. What about the earth where all life was created? The life form recently found deep beneath the Antarctic ice shelf[6] was not invented 2000 years ago with those religions, it was one of the earliest metamorphoses of life on earth. To consider these things does not show contempt for the six commandments but love and respect for the earth, our home.

To claim that we are here to multiply and have dominion over all animals and the earth itself is the ultimate hubris. We do not need to desert our religious life to reconsider the spiritual wisdom of that belief.

Our future is being compromised by the wedding between business and religion. Both Islam and Christianity preach unrestrained enterprise without consequence. The gentler sides of both religions have far greater logic and compassion, as well as a far greater chance of surviving as credos.

Our religions are sufficiently flexible to accommodate change. Sometimes change just needs a quasi-religious branding. For example, during the period called the Enlightenment, European philosophers, both religious and non-religious, campaigned for an end to the abomination of slavery and were eventually successful. In very recent times the campaign to recognise same-sex marriage was supported by many churches, and was not seen as heresy by enough Christians to prevent it passing through the parliaments of many European countries and their colonies.

A DIFFERENT WAY OF SEEING THE WORLD

The indications of a need for better regulation of our business world are all too obvious. In such wealthy countries as Australia, Britain and the United States, why are suicide and drug use so prevalent?[7] Why are people trying so hard to escape their lives? Why do they despair for our world? What is it about today's world that causes so many people to want to flee from it? Could it be the moral underpinnings of our approach to the earth?

Capitalists believe in profit. Many businesspeople see a tree or water and see only saleable goods; they do not believe in the forest or the river for itself. They spend national capital, they do not build it. This attitude to the national estate, the common wealth, robs the majority of people and rewards the selfish individual.

The system of capital exploitation has created our world of comfort and has spawned medicine and food technology, among other advances, but it hides skeletons in the cupboard. We know the spectres of poverty and drug use, environmental destruction and exponential division between rich and poor, but now we are witnessing systems of government that do not respect knowledge, and societies where conservative minds are ridiculed as if it is they who are destroying the traditions of state.

Indentured academics are part of this system and cannot pretend they are not profiting from it. Modern universities have been compelled by governments to focus their research on products and profit. Examining the workings of the natural world can be indulged only if a product such as Agent Orange or glyphosate is the outcome. Pure research, the pursuit of wonder, is seen as useless.

The world has received some enormous benefits from science and engineering, but not everything that a male engineer invents is good for the world. Bombing Hiroshima and Nagasaki was considered excusable on the pretext that it might have ended World War II, but we were yet to discover the true cost of the implementation of nuclear weapons. The firebombing of Dresden in that war was excused with the same reasoning. Engineers in the Mekong Delta felt that the tides were too disruptive of commerce and sought to rationalise them, resulting in enormous disruption to life that depended on tides. Fish stocks plummeted.[8] There was room in that decision-making process for an eight-year-old. Using Agent Orange to destroy forests in Vietnam during the Vietnam War was supposed to expose the enemy but did not. We destroyed the forests of a nation and still couldn't find the enemy. The Western world lost that war, and a generation of soldiers lost their entire nervous system.

Men are comfortable with collateral damage and use a domestic term to explain it: you can't make an omelette without breaking eggs.

Maybe if women had been in charge of those wars we would have seen better results. Maybe the women would have wondered what we were doing destroying other people's land. They might have said, 'Come on, let's go home and see how the chooks are going.'

That care would have been useful in the colonial period of Australia, when genuine philosophical thought was needed. Humanists keep telling me that, after the Enlightenment, everything changed in relation to Indigenous people. It did not. Lines of Aboriginal Australians were still being chained by the neck in Western Australia in 1958. The neck clamps were so well engineered that they were impossible to remove unless the prisoner's head was laid on an anvil and a spalling hammer and cold chisel were applied. Imagine your child listening to the hammer smashing down beside their head. How does a psyche endure the idea that another thought it right to chain you by the neck to a dozen of your people and leave you in the hot sun for a week, and if and when you were freed at last, the liberating method was to place your head on an anvil?

After World War II, new weapons testing was a macabre procedure. Australia was working with the British government to test nuclear weapons at Maralinga, in South Australia. It was considered a desert but Maralinga was home to the Tjarutja people, and the most desultory effort was made to inform them that atomic bombs would be dropped across their homeland. In the book *Women of the Centre*, Adele Pring records the stories of some of those people and the horrors they experienced. It took almost two decades for a whistleblower to expose this atrocity. What does it say about us, about our authorities, about our military historians and about our engineers? We cannot allow chemists and engineers open slather until they abide by the doctors' Hippocratic Oath, 'Do no harm'.

We need to enshrine the desire of people for a safe world. There has to be restraint and it must not be considered bad for business. In fact, it must be taught to our children as the most astute way of doing business. We need to inculcate an antidote to the 'Whatever it takes' approach so that young people, about to enter the business world, come armed with similar moral regulation as those in the medical profession. We need them to see environmental care and business honesty as points of honour, part of our cultural ethos, the essence of being human.

HOW MIGHT THE FUTURE LOOK?

When some Western nations decided that the threat of particular agricultural chemicals was too high to tolerate, they banned their use. Australia is still using many of those chemicals but there is movement here for us to control the use of such dangerous poisons.[9] Consumers in the capitalist system have power if they choose to use it.

The change in how we conduct agriculture has already begun. Some farmers on land where profits have been non-existent for decades have shifted to perennial Australian grasses and, although their overall income is down, they are now making a profit. Removing or reducing the costs of ploughing and chemicals has been the significant change. The grains find an easy market as more and more farmers switch to perennials. Some find it hard to break free from the habit of annual cropping and high stocking rates, but on a drying continent they realise that pattern is unsustainable.

So often we hear the country being blamed for a farmer's woes. Drought looms large in these conversations, but Aboriginal people allowed for low rainfall in their calculations of returns. Perhaps it is not so much drought, as the headlines declare, it is simply the wrong plants. The fish kills in the Murray-Darling are not caused by drought. They have been brought about by our assumption that all the water in any river belongs to humans, rich humans. The massive clouds of dust in the air every summer are not the result of drought but of wilful misuse of the land for short-term gain. The wildfires that destroy homes and kill people and livestock are not the result of drought but the direct culmination of our mismanagement of the common wealth forests.

Yumburra on the Wallagaraugh was a grazing property that used to be owned by an old mate of mine, George, a complete rascal. George supplemented his income by harvesting grey box and ironbark from his farm. Well, not always strictly within the boundaries of his property, but anyone can make a mistake! Because of this, there are very few old trees around the property. The forest is made up of mid-growth trees of approximately 800 millimetres radius and about 40 metres high, and the density is about 150–200 trees to the acre.

After the 2019–20 fires we had to rebuild sheds and add new ones, and we used many poles from the forest. We are planning to harvest all the small trees on our property and sell them to a milling contractor. Thinning our forest will provide us with income and help us reach our goal of having ten to twelve big trees to the acre, the pre-1788 principle of Aboriginal Australia.

The aim is for the forest to include a variety of types: grey box, red ironbark, stringybark and silvertop ash. At some point in the future we will run out of the forest thinnings, but if we combine this method with a concerted campaign to recycle timber then there should be no impediment to supply. Of course, this forest plan must be maintained for at least fifty years but we are doing it for the sake of our grandchildren and great-grandchildren. If we can prove that it works, it could be extended to other farms and hopefully, to the common wealth forests, we can create a sustainable timber industry, increase forest employment and make the forest safe from wildfire.

After the 2019–20 fires Yumburra received nice rain, and an abundance of grass appeared in the forest. With the canopy removed by crown fire, grasses flourished between the trees. As I described in Chapter 2, we had never seen this before and could not identify all the grasses we found, but it showed us that if we burnt judiciously and created a more open forest with fewer but bigger trees, we could get sunlight on the forest floor and bring back the old Aboriginal crops. After a few years the forest floor will be cleaner and easier for us to deploy our small Mandu harvester to pick up the new crops.

Imagine a national park being treated in the same fashion; we could be cropping in areas we haven't previously considered. I'm not suggesting that all parks can be utilised like this, but those consisting of more open country certainly lend themselves to this method. We won't see the disappearance of species that we are seeing with our current land use because our creatures evolved with a more open forest type.

Seeing the country differently doesn't mean we will see less of her; we're likely to see more as we learn to treat her like a park instead of a wilderness. Aboriginal people didn't see wilderness, we just saw our home. Her accessibility and comfort were our joy. Yuin people still travel their clan boundaries to protect and teach. It is one of the joys of culture to be out on country with the purpose of looking after her and hearing again the great stories of the life lived upon her.

If we are to make changes of this kind, we need to talk with the whole country about it. We must agree together to adopt the plan, not just have it foisted on a reluctant population. That means education across all levels. Schools are the obvious starting point but it must go beyond glossy pamphlets and propaganda from zealots. It has to be true education: problem, discussion, discussion, discussion, answer. Time is short, but real discussions, with all viewpoints considered, are crucial because the change has to be real. This is more important than anti-tobacco or skin cancer advertisements, we are talking about survival, not just recovery from an illness.

This program will require staff. People must be employed to oversee the return of forests to a safer model; fisheries must be planned and monitored and agricultural change needs to be supported, not left prey to the self-serving promotional campaigns of chemical companies. We have to show our dedication to Mother Earth by providing her with care. That care has to come from us, the people, not them, the salesmen.

It might seem impossible to change a world system where self-interest dominates and the rich parade their wealth in magazines they own. But if we work with our 0–8-year-olds and talk with them constantly about fairness and sharing and the responsibility of the fortunate to support the less fortunate, change is possible. And we need to talk with their fathers and mothers about taking a more generous, less profligate approach to consumption.

It might be that we as a country consider the formation of a treaty between Aboriginal and Torres Strait Islander people and non-Indigenous Australians. We may begin this process with acknowledging the modest plea of the Uluru Statement from the Heart. Former prime minister Malcolm Turnbull knocked it back before lunch on the day it was released to appease his right-wing parliamentary colleagues,[10] but they weren't appeased and the opportunity to have a perfectly decent conversation with our country was lost. Or maybe not lost, just delayed.

We only need to look at our country to see her hurt. We know we can do better than this, don't we? We know that solutions are there, tailor-made for our application. Swallow our pride, accept a more modest lifestyle which we may not even notice if we are truly committed to Mother Earth. A little less food, a little less water usage, fewer plastic trinkets, insisting on repairable household items. These measures are slight but all will make a difference to the health of the world.

Where are the leaders who can stand up to big business's backlash and the smear campaign that follows because businesspeople are jealous of their unsustainable profits? Will we provide those political leaders with armour to ward off such scurrilous campaigns? When will we stand up to the billionaires parading their horror of a tiny tax increase to compensate the common wealth for their use of our land? When will we turn our backs on greed and love our country for who she is?

The time has come to reckon with how history will judge us, for our actions or inactions. We cannot allow our country to be led by ideologues with such dangerous self-interest and disregard for the planet. If they just wanted to be rich we could probably tolerate it, but if they want their riches at the expense of the planet we cannot allow it. They might hate their grandchildren but we, the people, do not. We will raise them with a love of country.

ACKNOWLEDGEMENTS

My debts and gratitude for this book extend to the many people thanked in *The Biggest Estate* in 2011. I thank them again.

For this book I thank especially my wife Jan, my rock as always, and my friend Denis Tracey, tolerant critic. From Thames & Hudson Australia I thank Sally Heath and Elise Hassett. Extra help, mainly via email, came from Neil Barraclough, John Blay, Elizabeth Bor, Arch Cruttenden, Rob Foster, Tom Gara, David Joss, Darrell Lewis, Magali McDuffie, Joe Morrison, Jocelyn O'Neil, Bruce Pascoe, Katie Purvis, Henry Reynolds and Roger Underwood. Thank you all. – BG

I thank Uncle Max Harrison, Brad Steadman, Chris Harris, Terry Hayes, Nathan Lygon, Beth Gott, Louise Crisp, Bill Gammage, Rupert Gerritsen, Peter Latz, Lyn Harwood, Marnie Pascoe, Jack Pascoe, Annette Peisley, Ben Shewry, Bill Biddle, Ken Nash, Julie Kantor, Michael Gregg, the Federation of Traditional Owners Victoria and Yuin Gurandgi. – BP

IMAGE CREDITS

Inside covers *Warlpiri people burning spinifex*
© Mike Gillam/AUSCAPE
All rights reserved

Gospers Mountain fire at emergency level as heatwave continues
© David Gray/Stringer
Getty Images

ii *Flaming Trees*, 2020
© Danielle Gorogo
Photograph by Cher Breeze

48–51 Francis P MacCabe, *Tracing from Mr MacCabe's Plan of the Survey of the Genoa River, Part 2*, 1847. GIPPS54 Genoa River [microform], historical maps and plans collection, State Library Victoria.

62 Bread in coolamon. Kaytetye people, Barrow Creek, Desert East, Northern Territory, Australia, 1901. Spencer and Gillen Collection.
© Museums Victoria 2021
Photograph by Benjamin Healley

Bark container, grinding stone, bread. Ngukurr (Roper River), Eastern Arnhem Land, Northern Territory, Australia, 1911. Baldwin Spencer Collection.
© Museums Victorian 2021
Photograph by Benjamin Healley

IMAGE CREDITS

63 Detail of nardoo seeds, Australia.
© Museums Victoria 2021
Photograph by Benjamin Healley

Bread. Wambaya people, McArthur River, Gulf, Northern Territory, Australia, 1901. Spencer and Gillen Collection.
© Museums Victoria 2021
Photograph by Benjamin Healley

125 Thomas Scott Townsend (1812–1869), Copy of a tracing from Mr Boyd's map of the Edward and Murray rivers country, 1848. NSW State Archives, Surveyor General NRS 13889, Field Books NRS-13889-8-(2/8076.1)-O699, Tracing 41, c/- David Joss.

NOTES

FIRST KNOWLEDGES: AN INTRODUCTION
1 King O'Malley, a parliamentarian in the Australian House of Representatives, said in 1902, 'There is no scientific evidence that he [*sic*] is a human being at all': *Commonwealth Parliamentary Debates*, Commonwealth Franchise Bill, Second Reading, 23 April 1902, p. 11,929.
2 See David Abram, *Becoming Animal: An Earthly Cosmology*, Penguin Random House, New York, 2011.

1. PERSONAL PERSPECTIVES
1 Email to Bill Gammage, 3 February 2020.
2 Calla Wahlquist, 'Rio Tinto Blasts 46,000-Year-Old Aboriginal Site to Expand Iron Ore Mine', *The Guardian*, 26 May 2020.
3 See 'English Poor Laws', Wikipedia, 2021, <en.wikipedia.org/wiki/English_Poor_Laws>.
4 See, for example, 'Australian Agricultural and Rural Life: Life on the Land', State Library of New South Wales [website], n.d., <sl.nsw.gov.au/stories/australian-agricultural-and -rural-life/life-land>.
5 See, for example, Euan Ritchie & Adam Munn, 'Eat Locals: Swapping Sheep and Cattle for Kangaroos and Camels Could Help Our Environment', *The Conversation*, 23 May 2016.
6 John Vader, *Red Gold: The Tree that Built a Nation*, New Holland, Frenchs Forest, 2002.
7 Bernard O'Reilly, *Green Mountains*, Smith & Paterson, Brisbane, 1941; Don Watson, *The Bush: Travels in the Heart of Australia*, Penguin, Melbourne, 2014.
8 In Genesis 1:28, God grants humans 'dominion' over the Earth: 'And God blessed them, and God said unto them, Be fruitful, and multiply, and replenish the earth, and subdue it: and have dominion over the fish of the sea, and over the fowl of the air, and over every living thing that moveth upon the earth' (King James version).
9 See, for example, Andrew Darby, 'Fresh Bet on an Old Roughy', *Sydney Morning Herald*, 10 March 2015.
10 For more information, see 'Red Cedar', AgriFutures Australia, 2017, <agrifutures.com.au/farm-diversity/red-cedar/>.

2. LAND CARE
1 See, for example, KH Oedekoven, 'Forest History of the Near East', *Unasylva*, 17, 1963.

2   For a brief history of the 'Save the Whales' movement, see Sophy Grimshaw, 'Calls from the Deep: Do We Need to Save the Whales All Over Again?' *The Guardian*, 1 January 2021.
3   See Bill Gammage, *The Biggest Estate on Earth: How Aborigines Made Australia*, Allen & Unwin, Sydney, 2011.
4   Ben Knight, 'On Fire-Damaged Roads in Victoria, Army Crews Face the Daunting Job of Removing "Killer" Trees', *ABC News*, 12 January 2020; Miki Perkins, 'Conservation Watchdog Investigates: Is Bushfire Tree Removal "Overzealous"?' *The Age*, 5 March 2020.
5   G Singh, AP Kershaw & R Clark, 'Quaternary Vegetation and Fire History in Australia', in AM Gill, RH Groves & IR Noble (eds), *Fire and the Australian Biota*, Australian Academy of Science, Canberra, 1981, pp. 23–54.
6   Gammage, pp. 13–14.
7   See, for example, LT Carron, *A History of Forestry in Australia*, Australian National University Press, Canberra, 1985, p. 47, and Ian Bevege, 'The Railway Sleeper: A Critical Element of Early East Coast Bush Society and Forest Management', *Australian Forest History Society Newsletter*, 73, 2017, pp. 6–7.
8   Ruby Mitchell & Joshua Becker, 'Bush Food Industry Booms, But Only 1 Per Cent Is Produced by Indigenous People', *ABC News*, 19 January 2019.
9   Justice Olney's decision in 1998 that the Yorta Yorta native title claim had failed was because the land had been 'settled' by whites and the Yorta Yorta culture had been 'washed away by the tide of history'. Perhaps a new claim won't be so casually dismissed.
10 See, for example, Greg Martin, 'The Role of Small Ground-Foraging Mammals in Topsoil Health and Biodiversity: Implications to Management and Restoration', *Ecological Management & Restoration*, 4(2), 2003, pp. 114–19.
11 See, for example, Michelle Grattan, 'Dams Are Being Built, But They Are Private: Australia Institute', *The Conversation*, 8 October 2019.
12 The Murray-Darling Basin Authority has failed to balance the needs of farmers south of the massive cotton-farm dams and the needs of the environment. The idea of selling water, in some cases more than actually exists, has proven a horrible failure. See Kath Sullivan, 'Water Trading's "Unintended" Consequences across Australia's Southern Murray-Darling Basin', *ABC News*, 13 July 2019.
13 The duration of human habitation of the continent is now generally agreed to be 65,000 years, but recent research suggests that 120,000 years is probable: see Paul Daley, '"A Big Jump": People Might Have Lived in Australia Twice as Long as We Thought', *The Guardian*, 11 March 2019.
14 Peter Sutton & Keryn Walshe, *Farmers or Hunter-Gatherers? The* Dark Emu *Debate*, Melbourne University Press, Carlton, 2021, p. 148; John Hunter, *An Historical Journal of the Transactions at Port Jackson and Norfolk Island*, John Stockdale, London, 1793, p. 13.

15 See, for example, *The Journals of George Augustus Robinson, Chief Protector, Port Phillip Aboriginal Protectorate* (ed. Ian D Clark), vol. 2, 2nd edn, Heritage Matters, Melbourne, 2000, p. 326; Thomas Mitchell quoted in Beth Gott, 'Aboriginal Fire Management in SE Australia: Aims and Frequency', *Journal of Biogeography*, 32, 2005, p. 1204; Isaac Batey quoted in David Frankel, 'An Account of Aboriginal Use of the Yam Daisy', *The Artefact*, 7(1–2), 1982, pp. 43–4.
16 See, for example, JL Silcock, 'Aboriginal Translocations: The Intentional Propagation and Dispersal of Plants in Aboriginal Australia', *Journal of Ethnobiology*, 38(3), 2018, pp. 390–405.
17 Rupert Gerritsen, *Australia and the Origins of Agriculture*, British Archaeological Reports, Oxford, 2008; Bruce Pascoe, *Dark Emu: Aboriginal Australia and the Birth of Agriculture*, 2nd edn, Magabala Books, Broome, 2018.
18 Sutton & Walshe.
19 Paul Daley, 'As the Toll of Australia's Frontier Brutality Keeps Climbing, Truth Telling Is Long Overdue', *The Guardian*, 4 March 2019.
20 Chris Owen, 'How Western Australia's "Unofficial" Use of Neck Chains on Indigenous People Lasted 80 Years', *The Guardian*, 7 March 2021.
21 Bill Binks et al., *Snapshot of Australia's Agricultural Workforce*, Australian Bureau of Agricultural and Resource Economics and Sciences, Canberra, 2018, <https://doi.org/10.25814/5c09cefb3fec5>.

3. CULTIVATING COUNTRY

1 See, for example, Tobias Roberts, 'The Mindset of Monoculture', *Permaculture Research Institute*, 15 November 2017.
2 For more information, go to <blackduckfoods.org>.
3 George Grey quoted in Rupert Gerritsen, *Australia and the Origins of Agriculture*, British Archaeological Reports, Oxford, 2008, p. 33.
4 Thomas L Mitchell, *Journal of an Expedition into the Interior of Tropical Australia in Search of a Route from Sydney to the Gulf of Carpentaria*, Greenwood Press, New York, [1848] 1969, p. 90.
5 Isaac Batey quoted in David Frankel, 'An Account of Aboriginal Use of the Yam Daisy', *The Artefact*, 7(1–2), 1982, pp. 43–5.
6 Edward M Curr, *Recollections of Squatting in Victoria*, Libraries Board of South Australia, Adelaide, [1883] 1968; James Kirby, *Old Times in the Bush of Australia: Trials and Experiences of Early Bush Life in Victoria*, G Robertson & Co., Melbourne, 1897; Peter Beveridge, *The Aborigines of Victoria and Riverina*, ML Hutchinson, Melbourne, 1889; Isaac Batey, *Reminiscences of Settlement of the Melbourne and Sunbury District (1840–70)*, Royal Historical Society of Victoria Manuscripts Collection, MS 000035 (Box 016 [2-3]).
7 Kirby, p. 28.

8   Tim Low, 'The Vegetable Australia Gave the World', *Australian Geographic*, 17 October 2017.
9   In 1493 Pope Alexander VI issued a papal bull, or decree, called *Inter Caetera*, in which he divided the lands of the world, 'discovered and to be discovered', between the Spanish and Portuguese empires. The bull justified the taking of land from 'barbarous' nations if they didn't 'know' Jesus Christ and exhorted the spread of Christianity. *Inter Caetera* followed other papal orders of the 15th century that sanctioned the invasion of lands and enslavement of non-Christian peoples if they disagreed with the invaders' opinion about gods and spirituality. These papal bulls were the foundation of a 'doctrine of discovery', which allowed European nations to claim sovereignty over Indigenous peoples' lands. See 'Inter Caetera', Papal Encyclicals Online, n.d., <papalencyclicals.net/alex06/alex06inter.htm>; 'What Is the Doctrine of Discovery?' Doctrine of Discovery [website], 30 July 2018, <doctrineofdiscovery.org/what-is-the-doctrine-of-discovery/>; 'Conference Room Paper on the Doctrine of Discovery', 11th Session of the UN Permanent Forum on Indigenous Issues, 25 April 2012, <un.org/esa/socdev/unpfii/documents/2012/session-11-CRP2.pdf>.
10 Bronwyn Barkla, 'Warrigal Greens Are Tasty, Salty, and Covered in Tiny Balloon-Like Hairs', *The Conversation*, 24 February 2019.
11 See *The Journals of George Augustus Robinson, Chief Protector, Port Phillip Aboriginal Protectorate* (ed. Ian D Clark), vol. 4, 2nd edn, Heritage Matters, Melbourne, 2000.
12 See Nola O'Connor & Kathy Jones (comps), *A Journey Through Time: A Compilation of Stories of the Alexander Family*, self-published, 2003.
13 Edward M Curr, *The Australian Race: Its Origin, Languages, Customs, Place of Landing in Australia, and the Routes by Which It Spread Itself Over That Continent*, vol. 1, John Farnes, Melbourne, 1886, p. 240.
14 Bruce Pascoe, 'Bringing Back Aboriginal Industries', *Saturday Paper*, 6–12 March 2021; Tim Low, 'Australian Wild Foods: Ground Orchids – Salute to Saloop', *Australian Natural History*, 22(5), 1987, pp. 202–3.
15 Anna H Murphy et al., *National Recovery Plan for the Sunshine Diuris (Diuris fragrantissima)*, Department of Sustainability and Environment, Melbourne, 2008.
16 See Merlin Sheldrake, *Entangled Life: How Fungi Make Our Worlds, Change Our Minds and Shape Our Futures*, Random House, London, 2020.
17 See Philip A Clarke, *Discovering Aboriginal Plant Use: Journeys of an Australian Anthropologist*, Rosenberg, Dural, NSW, 2014.
18 See Gerritsen.
19 Mitchell, p. 90; Charles Sturt, *Narrative of an Expedition into Central Australia*, vol. 2, T&W Boone, 1849, p. 76.
20 See, for example, PAS Wurm et al., *Australian Native Rice: A New Sustainable Wild Food Enterprise*, RIRDC Publication No. 10/175, Rural Industries Research and Development Corporation, Canberra, 2011; and 'Commercialising Native Rice for Indigenous Enterprise Development: Agronomy and Value-Adding', *Future Food Systems*, 9 July 2020.

21 See 'Burke and Wills' Fatal Error', *ABC RN*, 7 August 2013; Peter Latz, *Pocket Bushtucker*, IAD Press, Alice Springs, 1999, p. 17.
22 Genelle Wuele & Felicity James, 'Indigenous Rock Shelter in Top End Pushes Australia's Human History Back to 65,000 Years', *ABC News*, 20 July 2017.
23 Anne & Leslie Dollin, 'Tracing Aboriginal Apiculture of Australian Native Bees in the Far North West', *The Australasian Beekeeper*, December 1986, pp. 118–21.

4. FUTURE FARMING

1 See, for example, 'Withholding Periods', Agriculture Victoria, 2021, <agriculture.vic.gov.au/farm-management/chemicals/managing-chemical-residues/withholding-periods>.
2 See, for example, James Dawson, *Australian Aborigines: The Languages and Customs of Several Tribes of Aborigines in the Western District of Victoria, Australia*, George Robertson, Melbourne, 1881.
3 For example, see John Lewis, 'Pieces of History', *Shepparton News*, 24 July 2010.
4 Rupert Gerritsen, *Australia and the Origins of Agriculture*, British Archaeological Reports, Oxford, 2008, p. 45.
5 Bryce D Stewart & Leigh Michael Howarth, 'Quantifying and Managing the Ecosystem Effects of Scallop Dredge Fisheries', in Sandra E Shumway & G Jay Parsons (eds), *Scallops: Biology, Ecology, Aquaculture, and Fisheries*, 3rd edn, Elsevier, Amsterdam, 2016, pp. 585–609.
6 Personal correspondence with fishermen from Apollo Bay.
7 See 'Southern Rock Lobster', GoodFish, n.d., <goodfish.org.au/species/southern-rock-lobster/>.
8 See Peter Kanowski & Neil McKenzie, 'Land: Soil', in *Australia State of the Environment 2011*, Australian Government Department of the Environment and Energy, Canberra, 2011, <soe.environment.gov.au/science/soe/2011-report/5-land/2-state-and-trends/2-2-soil>.
9 See Monique Ross & Annabelle Quince, 'The History of Fire in Australia – and How It Can Help Us Face the Bushfires of the Future', *ABC News*, 10 February 2020.

5. COUNTRY

1 Edward M Curr, *Recollections of Squatting in Victoria*, Libraries Board of South Australia, Adelaide, [1883] 1968, pp. 188–90.
2 1 Jun 1835. Thomas L Mitchell, *Three Expeditions into the Interior of Eastern Australia*, vol. 1, Libraries Board of South Australia, Adelaide, [1839] 1965, p. 222.
3 Martuwarra RiverOfLife, Magali McDuffie & Anne Poelina, 'Martuwarra Country: A Historical Perspective (1838–Present)', *Nulungu Research Papers*, 5, 2020, pp. 19–28, quote p. 28, c/- Magali McDuffie.
4 Simpson Newland, 'Annual Address', *Journal of the Royal Geographical Society of Australasia*, South Australian Branch, 22, 1921, p. 3.

5   Bill Gammage, 'Galahs', *Australian Historical Studies*, 40(3), Sep 2009, pp. 275–93.
6   Margaret Kiddle, *Men of Yesterday: A Social History of the Western District of Victoria, 1834–1890*, Melbourne University Press, Melbourne, [1961] 1967, p. 182.
7   See for example Mike Foley, 'Why Is Australia a Global Leader in Wildlife Extinctions?' *Sydney Morning Herald*, 20 July 2020.
8   George Bennett, *Wanderings in New South Wales, Batavia, Pedir Coast, Singapore, and China*, vol. 1, Libraries Board of South Australia, Adelaide, [1834] 1967, p. 259.
9   TGH Strehlow, *Aranda Traditions*, Melbourne University Press, Melbourne, 1947, pp. 30–1.
10 10 Oct – 3 Nov 1830. NJB Plomley (ed.), *Friendly Mission: The Tasmanian Journals and Papers of George Augustus Robinson 1829–1834*, Tasmanian Historical Research Association, Hobart, 1966, pp. 245–66, 438–9nn44, 51; Bill Gammage, *The Biggest Estate on Earth: How Aborigines Made Australia*, Allen & Unwin, Sydney, 2011, pp. 137–8.
11 Regrettably, I don't know the speaker's name. He spoke on NITV on 6 Dec 2015.
12 Thomas Francis Bride (ed.), *Letters from Victorian Pioneers*, Currey O'Neil, Melbourne, [1898] 1983, pp. 426–7.
13 Alan E Newsome, 'The Eco-Mythology of the Red Kangaroo in Central Australia', *Mankind*, 12(4), 1980, pp. 327–33.

6. AN ANCIENT ALLIANCE

1   Charles Sturt, *Two Expeditions into the Interior of Southern Australia*, vol. 1, Public Library of South Australia, Adelaide, [1833] 1963, p. xxviii.
2   28 Jan 1833. Ronald C Gunn, 'Account of a Journey Inland from Launceston to Deloraine' (pp. 6–7), Tasmanian Archives: Copies of Correspondence of RC Gunn, NS 1313/1/1 [microform].
3   Dymphna Clark (trans. & ed.), *New Holland Journal: November 1833–October 1834* (Charles von Hügel), Melbourne University Press, Melbourne, 1994, pp. 279–80.
4   26 May 1827. Ida Lee, *Early Explorers in Australia*, Methuen, London, 1925, p. 558.
5   William L Morton, 'Notes of a Recent Personal Visit to the Unoccupied Northern District of Queensland', *Transactions of the Philosophical Institute of Victoria*, 4, 1859, p. 197.
6   Edward J Eyre, *Journals of Expeditions of Discovery into Central Australia*, vol. 1, Libraries Board of South Australia, Adelaide, [1845] 1964, p. 35.
7   Charles Sturt, *Narrative of an Expedition into Central Australia*, vol. 2, Libraries Board of South Australia, Adelaide, [1849] 1965, pp. 229–30.
8   J Stuwe, 'The Role of Fire in Ground Flora Ecology', *Victorian Naturalist*, 111, 1994, pp. 93–5.
9   David MJS Bowman, 'The Impact of Aboriginal Landscape Burning on the Australian Biota', *New Phytologist*, 140(3), 1998, pp. 392–4.

10. JMB Smith (ed.), *A History of Australasian Vegetation*, McGraw-Hill, Sydney, 1982, p. 142.
11. *South Australian Register*, 22 Jun 1839, p. 4, c/- Tom Gara.
12. Eric K Webb (ed.), *Windows on Meteorology: Australian Perspective*, CSIRO Publishing, Melbourne, 1997, pp. 9–10.
13. George Vancouver, *A Voyage of Discovery to the North Pacific Ocean and Round the World, 1791–1795*, vol. 1, rev. edn, The Hakluyt Society, London, [1801] 1984, p. 355.
14. 29 Nov 1828. Henry Hellyer report, Tasmanian Archives: microfilm Z3232, Tasmanian Archival Estrays, Dixson Library, Sydney.
15. David R Moore, *Islanders and Aborigines at Cape York*, AIAS, Canberra, 1979, p. 127.
16. Rhys Jones, 'Fire-Stick Farming', *Australian Natural History*, 16(7), Sep 1969, pp. 224–8.
17. George 'Mac' Core to Bruce Simpson & Bill Gammage, in the *Drovers Oral History Project* [sound recording], Charters Towers (Qld), 6 Oct 2002, <nla.gov.au/nla.obj-221267197>.
18. 13 Sep 1846. Thomas L Mitchell, *Journal of an Expedition into the Interior of Tropical Australia*, London, 1848, pp. 305–6.
19. Edward M Curr, *Recollections of Squatting in Victoria*, Libraries Board of South Australia, Adelaide, [1883] 1968, p. 430.
20. Robert C Ellis, 'The Relationships among Eucalypt Forest, Grassland and Rainforest in a Highland Area in North-Eastern Tasmania', *Australian Journal of Ecology*, 10(3), 1985, pp. 297–314; Ian Thomas, 'The Holocene Archaeology and Palaeoecology of Northeastern Tasmania, Australia', PhD thesis, University of Tasmania, 1991; Bill Mollison to Bill Gammage, Sisters Creek (Tas), 12 Feb 2002.
21. Mitchell, p. 412.
22. François Péron, *A Voyage of Discovery to the Southern Hemisphere*, Walsh & Walsh, Melbourne, [1809] 1975, p. 331.
23. 27 Nov 1826. Helen Rosenman (trans. & ed.), *An Account in Two Volumes of Two Voyages to the South Seas* (Jules Dumont d'Urville), Melbourne University Press, Melbourne, 1987, p. 66.
24. *South Australian Register*, 26 Jun 1841, p. 3, c/- Tom Gara.
25. Alfred W Howitt, 'The Eucalypts of Gippsland', *Transactions of the Royal Society of Victoria*, 2(1), 1890, pp. 109, 112–13.
26. David Ward, 'Trouble in the Tuart: A Brief Fire History', Department of Conservation and Land Management (CALM), Perth, 2000, p. 1; Oct 1872. Ernest Giles, *Australia Twice Traversed: The Romance of Exploration*, Hesperian Press, Perth, [1889] 1995, p. 36.
27. 2 Aug 1845. Ludwig Leichhardt, *Journal of an Overland Expedition in Australia*, Libraries Board of South Australia, Adelaide, [1847] 1964, pp. 354–5.
28. Eyre, vol. 2, p. 357.
29. Deborah Bird Rose (ed.), *Country in Flames: Proceedings of the 1994 Symposium on Biodiversity and Fire in North Australia*, Department of the Environment, Sport and Territories, Canberra, 1995, p. 27.

30 Jeremy Russell-Smith et al., 'Aboriginal Resource Utilization and Fire Management Practice in Western Arnhem Land, Monsoonal Northern Australia: Notes for Prehistory, Lessons for the Future', *Human Ecology*, 25(2), 1997, p. 174.
31 Jeremy Russell-Smith, Peter Whitehead & Peter Cooke (eds), *Culture, Ecology and Economy of Fire Management in North Australian Savannas: Rekindling the Wurrk Tradition*, CSIRO Publishing, Melbourne, 2009, pp. 95, 110.
32 R Bliege Bird et al., 'The "Fire Stick Farming" Hypothesis: Australian Aboriginal Foraging Strategies, Biodiversity, and Anthropogenic Fire Mosaics', *Proceedings of the National Academy of Sciences of the United States of America*, 105(39), 2008, p. 14,797.
33 George F Moore, *Diary of Ten Years Eventful Life of an Early Settler in Western Australia*, London, 1884, pp. 12, 39, 45, 60, 81.

7. HOLDING THE SPARK

1 G Kelly, 'Karla Wongi: Fire Talk', in D Gough (ed.), *Fire: The Force of Life* (*Landscope*), CALM, Perth, 2000, p. 11.
2 Ethel Hassell, 'Notes on the Ethnology of the Wheelman Tribe of Southwestern Australia', *Anthropos*, 31, 1936, pp. 698–700.
3 Marcia Langton, *Burning Questions: Emerging Environmental Issues for Indigenous Peoples in Northern Australia*, Centre for Indigenous Natural and Cultural Resource Management, Northern Territory University, Darwin, 1998, p. 1.
4 Alan Rumsey & James Weiner (eds), *Emplaced Myth: Space, Narrative, and Knowledge in Aboriginal Australia and Papua New Guinea*, University of Hawaii Press, Honolulu, 2001, p. 109.
5 Nov 1840. John Lort Stokes, *Discoveries in Australia*, vol. 2, Libraries Board of South Australia, Adelaide, [1846] 1969, p. 228.
6 Lynn Baker (comp.), *Mingkiri: A Natural History of Uluru by the Mutitjulu Community* (Edith Richards et al.), IAD Press, Alice Springs, 1996, pp. 49–50.
7 3 Nov 1836. Thomas L Mitchell, *Three Expeditions into the Interior of Eastern Australia*, vol. 2, Libraries Board of South Australia, Adelaide, [1839] 1965, p. 328.
8 John Banks, 'Trees: The Silent Fire Historians', *Bogong*, 18, 1997, pp. 11–12.
9 Oscar de Satge, *Pages from the Journal of a Queensland Squatter*, Hurst & Blackett, London, 1901, p. 142.
10 William A Brodribb, *Recollections of an Australian Squatter*, Queensberry Hill Press, Melbourne, [1883] 1976, p. 24.
11 Lynette C McLoughlin, 'Season of Burning in the Sydney Region', *Australian Journal of Ecology*, 23(4), 1998, pp. 393–4.
12 Frank Young to Bill Gammage, 24 Aug 2002.
13 R Bliege Bird et al., 'The "Fire Stick Farming" Hypothesis: Australian Aboriginal Foraging Strategies, Biodiversity, and Anthropogenic Fire Mosaics',

Proceedings of the National Academy of Sciences of the United States of America, 105(39), 2008, p. 14,797.
14 8 Oct 1872. Ernest Giles, *Australia Twice Traversed: The Romance of Exploration*, Hesperian Press, Perth, [1889] 1995, p. 42.
15 Derek J Mulvaney & Peter White (eds), *Australians to 1788*, Fairfax, Syme & Weldon, Sydney, 1987, p. 223.
16 Tom Vigilante, 'Analysis of Explorers' Records of Aboriginal Landscape Burning in the Kimberley', *Australian Geographical Studies*, 39(2), 2001, pp. 135, 143–4.
17 Geoffrey Cary, David Lindenmayer & Stephen Dovers, *Australia Burning: Fire Ecology, Policy and Management Issues*, CSIRO Publishing, Melbourne, 2003, p. 199.
18 Robert Dundas Murray, *A Summer in Port Phillip*, Edinburgh, 1843, pp. 199–200.
19 Ross A Bradstock, Jann E Williams & A Malcolm Gill, *Flammable Australia: The Fire Regimes and Biodiverstiy of a Continent*, Cambridge University Press, Cambridge, 2002, p. 412; Ross A Bradstock, Michael Bedward, A Malcolm Gill & JS Cohn, 'Which Mosaic? A Landscape Ecological Approach for Evaluating Interactions Between Fire Regimes, Habitat and Animals', *Wildlife Research*, 32(5), 2005, pp. 409–23.
20 Peta-Marie Standley, 'The Importance of Campfires to Effective Conservation', PhD thesis, James Cook University, 2019, p. 166.
21 Gough, p. 24.
22 Mulvaney & White, pp. 221, 223.
23 BS Hetzel & HJ Frith (eds), *The Nutrition of Aborigines in Relation to the Ecosystem of Central Australia*, CSIRO, Melbourne, 1978, p. 78.
24 John Bradley to Bill Gammage, 11 Jul 2001.
25 25–26 Jan 1802. Elizabeth de Quincey, *The History of Mount Wellington: A Tasmanian Sketchbook*, self-published, Hobart, 1987, p. 29.
26 Mary Thomas, *The Diaries and Letters of Mary Thomas (1836–1866)*, ed. Evan Kyffin Thomas, WK Thomas & Co., Adelaide, 1925, p. 123, c/- Tom Gara.
27 George French Angas, *Savage Life and Scenes in Australia and New Zealand*, vol. 1, Reed, Wellington, NZ, [1847] 1968, p. 43, c/- Tom Gara.
28 *South Australian Register*, 27 Mar 1841, p. 4, c/- Tom Gara.
29 Scott Nind, 'Description of the Natives of King George's Sound (Swan River Colony) and Adjoining Country', *Journal of the Royal Geographical Society of London*, 1, 1830–31, p. 28.
30 JRB Love, *Stone-Age Bushmen of Today: Life and Adventure among a Tribe of Savages in North-Western Australia*, Blackie & Son, London, 1936, p. 85.
31 Donald F Thomson, 'Arnhem Land: Explorations among an Unknown People', *Geographical Journal*, 113, 1949, p. 7.
32 Quoted in Iain McCalman, *The Reef: A Passionate History*, Penguin, Melbourne, 2013, p. 153.

33 Deborah Bird Rose, *Nourishing Terrains: Australian Aboriginal Views of Landscape and Wilderness*, Australian Heritage Commission, Canberra, 1996, p. 67.
34 *The Border Watch*, 23 Nov 1876, c/- Darrell Lewis.
35 Edward M Curr, *Recollections of Squatting in Victoria*, Libraries Board of South Australia, Adelaide, [1883] 1968, pp. 170, 188–90 (map).
36 David Joss emails to Bill Gammage, 22–23 May 2012.
37 Aug 1831. NJB Plomley (ed.), *Friendly Mission: The Tasmanian Journals and Papers of George Augustus Robinson 1829–1834*, Tasmanian Historical Research Association, Hobart, 1966, p. 398.
38 BJ McKaige, RJ Williams & WM Waggitt (comps), *Bushfire '97: Proceedings Australian Bushfire Conference* [8–10 Jul 1997, Plaza Hotel, Darwin], CSIRO Tropical Ecosystems Research Centre, Darwin, 1997, p. 77; CD Haynes, MG Ridpath & MAJ Williams (eds), *Monsoonal Australia: Landscape, Ecology and Man in the Northern Lowlands*, AA Balkema, Rotterdam, NL, 1991, p. 69.
39 Langton, p. 1.
40 Deborah Bird Rose (ed.), *Country in Flames: Proceedings of the 1994 Symposium on Biodiversity and Fire in North Australia*, Department of the Environment, Sport and Territories, Canberra, 1995, p. 26.

1788 FIRE NOTES

1 Mary Gilmore, *Old Days, Old Ways*, Angus & Robertson, Sydney, 1934, pp. 220–1.

8. BABES IN THE WOOD

1 Ray Parkin, *H.M. Bark Endeavour: Her Place in Australian History*, Melbourne University Press, Melbourne, 1997, pp. 178, 188–9.
2 Nov 1826. Robert Dawson, *The Present State of Australia*, Alburgh, UK, [1830] 1987, pp. 108–9.
3 Bill Gammage, *The Biggest Estate on Earth: How Aborigines Made Australia*, Allen & Unwin, Sydney, 2011, pp. 14–17.
4 *South Australian Gazette and Colonial Register*, 9 Mar 1839, p. 7, c/- Elizabeth Bor.
5 *Adelaide Observer*, 17 Mar 1855, 5 Apr 1856, c/- Tom Gara.
6 Neil Burrows & Ian Abbott (eds), *Fire in Ecosystems of South-West Western Australia: Impacts and Management*, Backhuys Publishers, Leiden, NL, 2003, p. 120.
7 Mar 1846. David Ward, 'Fire, Flogging, Measles and Grass: Nineteenth Century Land Use Conflict in South-Western Australia', CALM, Perth, 1998, pp. 11–12.
8 Edward M Curr, *The Australian Race: Its Origin, Languages, Customs, Place of Landing in Australia, and the Routes by Which It Spread Itself Over That Continent*, vol. 3, John Ferres, Government Printer, Melbourne, 1887, p. 21, c/- Henry Reynolds & Jocelyn O'Neil.
9 Victor Steffensen, *Fire Country: How Indigenous Fire Management Could Help Save Australia*, Hardie Grant, Melbourne, 2020, pp. 20, 25–32.

10 TM Perry, *Australia's First Frontier: The Spread of Settlement in New South Wales, 1788–1829*, Melbourne University Press, Melbourne, 1963, p. 28.
11 1846. Thomas L Mitchell, *Journal of an Expedition into the Interior of Tropical Australia*, London, 1848, p. 413.
12 LP Hunt & R Sinclair (eds), *Focus on the Future – The Heat Is On! Proceedings of the 9th Australian Rangeland Society Biennial Conference* [24–27 Sep 1996, Port Augusta, South Australia], Australian Rangeland Society, Perth, 1996, pp. 62–3; EH Norris, PB Mitchell & DM Hart, 'Vegetation Changes in the Pilliga Forests: A Preliminary Evaluation of the Evidence', *Vegetatio*, 91, 1991, p. 216.
13 Gammage, pp. 318–20.
14 Judith Wright, *The Cry for the Dead*, Oxford University Press, Melbourne, 1981, pp. 12–13, 277.
15 Eric Rolls, *A Million Wild Acres*, Penguin, Melbourne, 1984, pp. 1, 70.
16 Dec 1836. WSP Bunbury & WP Morrell (eds), *Early Days in Western Australia*, Oxford University Press, London, 1930, pp. 105–6.
17 JC Hamilton, *Pioneering Days in Western Victoria*, Exchange Press, Melbourne, c. 1913, p. 37.
18 David Ward, 'Trouble in the Tuart: A Brief Fire History', CALM, Perth, 2000, p. 11.
19 Simpson Newland, 'Annual Address', *Journal of the Royal Geographical Society of Australasia*, South Australian Branch, 22, 1921, p. 3.
20 Lynn Baker (comp.), *Mingkiri: A Natural History of Uluru by the Mutitjulu Community* (Edith Richards et al.), IAD Press, Alice Springs, 1996, p. 49.
21 Norman A Wakefield, 'Bushfire Frequency and Vegetational Change in South-Eastern Australian Forests', *Victorian Naturalist*, 87, 1970, pp. 152–8.
22 David MJS Bowman & WJ Panton, 'Decline of *Callitris intratropica*', *Journal of Biogeography*, 20(4), 1993, pp. 373, 380.
23 Tom Griffiths, *Forests of Ash: An Environmental History*, Cambridge University Press, Port Melbourne, 2001, pp. 23–7.
24 Victoria, Royal Commission, *Report of the Royal Commission to Inquire into the Causes of and Measures Taken to Prevent the Bush Fires of January, 1939 …*, Government Printer, Melbourne, 1939, pp. 7, 11, 21, 31.
25 Parkin, p. 369.
26 Victoria, Royal Commission, *Report* (1939), pp. 16, 31.
27 Victoria, Royal Commission, *Report of the Royal Commission to Inquire into the Place of Origin and the Causes of the Fires which Commenced at Yallourn on the 14th Day of February, 1944 …*, HE Daw, Government Printer, Melbourne, 1944, p. 8.
28 'The Truth about Fuel Reduction Burning', Bushfire Front, accessed 16 Sep 2020, <bushfirefront.org.au/the-truth-about-fuel-reduction-burning/>; Phil Cheney, David Packham & Tim Malseed, 'The Royal Commission into National Natural Disaster Arrangements', *The Volunteer Fire Fighter*, 12(1), 2020, p. 7.
29 Roger Underwood to Bill Gammage, 24 Dec 2020.
30 Michael Holton, 'President's Report', *The Volunteer Fire Fighter*, 12(1), 2020, p. 3.

31 Television program – regrettably, I don't know the program's name or the date it was broadcast; Michael Gordon, 'The Forgotten Lands', *The Age*, 16 Aug 2014, pp. 28–30.
32 Lynette C McLoughlin, 'Season of Burning in the Sydney Region', *Australian Journal of Ecology*, 23(4), 1998, p. 393.
33 Roger Underwood to Bill Gammage, 25 Jan 2020.
34 Bushfire Front, 16 Sep 2020.
35 Nick O'Malley, 'Survey Finds 71 per cent of Koala Populations Died in Some NSW Fires', *Sydney Morning Herald*, 5 September 2020.
36 Stan Gorton, 'Kangaroo Island Koala Numbers Estimated to Be Down to 8500 from 48,000 Before Bushfires', *The Islander*, 14 December 2020.
37 Peter Hannam, 'Guardians of the Wollemi Pine', *Sydney Morning Herald*, 29 May 2021, p. 19, c/- Arch Cruttenden.

9. POOR FELLA MY COUNTRY

1 Francis P MacCabe, *Tracing from Mr MacCabe's Plan of the Survey of the Genoa River, Part 2*, 1847. GIPPS54 Genoa River [microform], historical maps and plans collection, State Library Victoria.
2 'Fire in East Gippsland: Recollections of John Mulligan', The Volunteer Fire Fighters Association (VFFA), 3 Feb 2020, <volunteerfirefighters.org.au/fire-in-east-gippsland-recollections-of-john-mulligan>.
3 VFFA, 3 Feb 2020; Vic Jurskis, 'Ex-FRNSW Fire Chief Joins Climate Crazies', VFFA, 21 Jan 2019, <volunteerfirefighters.org.au/ex-frnsw-fire-chief-joins-climate-crazies>.
4 Pat Anderson et al., *Continent Aflame: Responses to an Australian Catastrophe*, Palaver, Melbourne, 2020, p. 150.
5 Australia, Royal Commission, *Royal Commission into National Natural Disaster Arrangements: Report*, Commonwealth of Australia, Canberra, 2020, para 17.42.
6 Victoria, Royal Commission, *Report of the Royal Commission to Inquire into the Causes of and Measures Taken to Prevent the Bush Fires of January, 1939 ...*, Government Printer, Melbourne, 1939, p. 14.
7 *ANU Reporter*, 51(1), 2020, p. 9.
8 Australia, Royal Commission, *Report* (2020), p. 59.
9 *Cassell's Illustrated Family Paper*, 4 Feb 1854, p. 46, c/- John Blay.
10 Victoria, Royal Commission, *Report* (1939), p. 5.
11 Roy Ellen & Katsuyoshi Fukui (eds), *Redefining Nature: Ecology, Culture, and Domestication*, Berg Publishers, Oxford, 1996, pp. 177–81.
12 Fred Watson (ed.), *Historical Records of Australia*, series 4, vol. 1, Government Printer, Sydney, 1914–22, p. 414.
13 5 Jan 1688. William Dampier, *A New Voyage Round the World*, London, 1696, pp. 464–6.

14 7 Nov 1838. Charles Rowley, *The Destruction of Aboriginal Society*, Penguin, Melbourne, 1972, p. 37.
15 Thomas Fuller (*New York Times*) to Bill Gammage, 11 Jan 2020.
16 See for example Mike Foley, 'Why Is Australia a Global Leader in Wildlife Extinctions?' *Sydney Morning Herald*, 20 July 2020.
17 Victoria, Royal Commission, *Report* (1939), p. 6.
18 Australia, Royal Commission, *Report* (2020), p. 21, para 16.
19 For Aboriginal organisations managing fire in 2020, see Australia, Royal Commission, *Report* (2020), pp. 387–97.

10. HOW WE MIGHT LOVE MOTHER EARTH MORE

1 Matt Brann & Hugh Hogan, 'Woodchip Price in Australia Through the Roof Thanks to Asian Demand', *ABC News*, 8 July 2019.
2 See <agriculture.gov.au/forestry> for details.
3 Tansy Hoskins, 'Cotton Production Linked to Images of the Dried Up Aral Sea Basin', *The Guardian*, 2 October 2014.
4 Calla Wahlquist, 'Rio Tinto Blasts 46,000-Year-Old Aboriginal Site to Expand Iron Ore Mine', *The Guardian*, 26 May 2020.
5 Marcus Strom & Brendan Foster, 'Burrup Peninsula Aboriginal Rock Art Could Be Given World Heritage Status', *WA Today*, 27 February 2017.
6 Adam Vaughan, 'Life Found Beneath Antarctic Ice Sheet "Shouldn't Be There"', *New Scientist*, 15 February 2021.
7 See, for example, *Suicide in the World: Global Health Estimates*, World Health Organization, 2019; Hannah Ritchie & Max Roser, 'Drug Use', Our World in Data, 2019, <ourworldindata.org/drug-use>.
8 Emmy Sasipornkarn, 'A Dam-Building Race Threatens the Mekong River', *Deutsche Welle*, 16 August 2018.
9 See, for example, Jess Davis, 'One Sip of Herbicide Containing Paraquat Could Kill, But Farmers Don't Want It Banned', *ABC News*, 31 March 2021.
10 Calla Wahlquist, 'Indigenous Voice Proposal "Not Desirable", Says Turnbull', *The Guardian*, 26 October 2017.

FURTHER READING

Evans, Matthew, *Soil: The Incredible Story of What Keeps the Earth, and Us, Healthy*, Murdoch Books, Sydney, 2021.

Gammage, Bill, *The Biggest Estate on Earth: How Aborigines Made Australia*, Allen & Unwin, Sydney, 2011.

O'Reilly, Bernard, *Green Mountains*, Smith & Paterson, Brisbane, 1941.

Pyne, Stephen, *The Still-Burning Bush*, Scribe, Melbourne, 2020.

Rolls, Eric, *A Million Wild Acres*, Penguin, Melbourne, 1984.

Sheldrake, Merlin, *Entangled Life: How Fungi Make Our Worlds, Change Our Minds and Shape Our Futures*, Random House, London, 2020.

Steffensen, Victor, *Fire Country: How Indigenous Fire Management Could Help Save Australia*, Hardie Grant, Melbourne, 2020.

Watson, Don, *The Bush: Travels in the Heart of Australia*, Penguin, Melbourne, 2014.

INDEX

Page numbers in **bold** refer to maps, captions or images.

Aboriginal peoples/groups/clans
 Anangu (*Anungu*), 110–11, 139–40
 of Arnhem Land, 126
 of Arnhem Land plateau, 104, 115
 Arrernte (Aranda), 115
 Bidwell, 47
 Bidwell-Maap, 52
 Bundjalung, 172
 of Cape York, 115, 118
 Ganai, 42, 45
 Guugu Yimithirr, 143
 Gweagal, 171
 Kaurna, 120
 Kaytetye, **62**
 Kuku Thaypan, 118
 Martu, 104, 115
 Murri, 60
 Tjarutja, 179
 Wailwan, 40
 Wambaya, **63**
 of West Arnhem, 104
 Yanyuwa, 103, 116, 119
 Yolŋu, 122
 Yorta Yorta, 27
 Yuin, 24, 47, 57, 172, 183
Abram, David, 5, 7

Alexander, Robert, 52
Allen, Thomas, 94
Angas, GF, 120
Australasian Beekeeper (journal), 65
Australia and history
 history wars, 2, 3
 landscape at invasion, 5
 language and terminology, 3, 4, 11, 61
 past of and truth-telling, 2; debates over sovereignty, treaty, 3
 reconciliation, 6
 and terra nullius, 4, 45, 161, 162

Banks, John, 112–13
Banks, Joseph, 133, 134
Barraclough, Neil, 142
Batey, Isaac, 39
Bennett, George, 79
Beveridge, Peter, 39, 40
Bill, Uncle, 57
Bowler, Jim, 31
Bunbury, HW, 138
Burke, Robert O'Hara, 59

capitalism. *See* loving Mother Earth; science and technology
Clarke, Uncle Banjo, 72

INDEX

colonial/newcomer land and resource practices since 1788, 1, 2, 5, 29
  and Aboriginal land management methods, 7, 25, 26, 29, 31, 32, 37, 39, 77, 154; knowledge lost, 127, 132; sustainability, 14–15, 19
  and attempts to control nature, 12, 20, 30; Northern Hemisphere methods, 29, 35, 68
  and conservation efforts, 21
  destructive, 1, 2, 3, 39, 40, 41, 42, 77; degradation of water sources, land, 78, 82, 136–7; habitat loss, 53, 58, 77, 81, 162; introduced (hard-hoofed) animals, 16, 41, 53–4, 58, 67, 68, 115, 127, (and chemicals), 69; loss of native grasses, 80, 81, 139; salinity, 78–9; soil erosion, compaction, 73, 78, 79
  farming crises, 30; insect plagues, 101
  fear of the land, 5, 20, 26; narrative of hardship, 24–5
  fire, fuel loads, 29, 52, 141; build-up of fuel loads, 153–5, 157, 159, 160, 162, 164; and climate change, 132, 146, 155, 156, 158; control burning, 155–6, 160, 165; fear of fire, 25, 119, 163; fire as ally, 160, 165; firefighting methods, 150–1, 155, 159–60, (and failure), 155, 164; fuel reduction burning, 11, 52, 132, 144–7, 150, 153, 156, 158, 160, (and 1788 fire), 147, 151; ignorance, 162; indiscreet use of fire, 138, 140, (impacts), 140, 147; little use of fire, 136–8, 143, 149, 154; 'no fire' as normal, 136; and prevention of bushfires, 142–3, 146, 160, (backburning), 146; and species protection, 147–8, 149, 150, 151; suggested approach to fire, 164–6, (with Aboriginal experts), 165, 166–7; and white Australian history, 155, 156–8, 161
  forestry, 22, 24, 25; and fuel loads, 25, 80, 153, 154, 162; loss of jobs, 170–1
  introduced crops, plants, pests, diseases, tree species, 58, 59, 76–7, 79, 81, 146, 164, 190; feral animals, 162, 164
  land management: degradation, 16–17, 24, 76, 81, 101, 148, 175; ignorance, 163; impacts, 17, 18, 79; logging, 22, 148; rape and pillage, 6, 18; for settlements, 78; trees seen as enemies, 20, 23
  parks and undergrowth, 52, 80
  preventing Aboriginal management, burning, 25, 33, 134, 135–6, 139, 154–5, 162
  rivers and streams: drainage, 79; flows altered, 79
  seafood: overfishing, 17, 18, 71–3
  species extinctions, reductions, 18, 76, 77, 78, 148–9, 162, 163–4; Australia's record, 78; endangered species, 77, 78
  tree numbers, distribution, 80

wetlands, 40–1, 42; and birdlife, 41–2; reduced, 79
see also natural disasters; science and technology
colonisation/invasion, 68
  early impressions of land, 25, 29, 39, 133, 138; abundance of animals, birds, fish, 76; fecundity of regions, 39, 40, 76, 77; herbs, tubers, lilies, orchids, 81, (and fire), 81; misconceptions, ignorance, 111–12, 133–4, 161–2
  and history books, 16
  impact on Indigenous societies, 7, 16, 134, 135, 162; dispersal, removal, 126, 136, 138, 139, 168; habitat loss, 53, 58; intimidation, 33; massacres, stray killings, 33, 52, 162; use of neck chains, 33–4, 179
  and justification, 45; contested Aboriginal occupation, 45, 46; a 'hierarchy' of humans, 32, 45; terra nullius, 45, 161, 162
  and views of Aboriginal people, 3, 161, 189; agricultural management, 31, 75, 88, 90, 100; appreciation of fire regimes, 136–9; as nomads, 4
  and wilderness, 162
  see also natural disasters; science and technology
Cook, James, 43, 133, 134
  Endeavour River camp, 143
  warrigal greens, 42, 43
Core, Mac, 98

Country
  ancestral and spiritual dimensions, 5, 81, 82, 83–4; ritual, 162; totems, relationships, 81, 84
  central to Indigenous people, 1, 24; care for, 1, 5–6, 83, 159, (despite risk), 83; Country as a companion, 5; Country as mother, 5, 27, 162
  and changes (non-Indigenous) wrought since 1788, 76–81
  knowledge resides in, 2
  maintaining Country, 25, 29, 102–3; knowledge of, 128; leaving it as you found it, 83, 105; and mobility, 103; shaping it, 95, 97
  and native title claims, 27, 190
  people as part of Country, 5, 83; affection for Country, 82, 159; displaced, 78
  and story, 82
  totems and obligation, 84–5; and habitats, 85, 97, 102, 128, 148
  as way of seeing, relating to the world, 5
  see also colonial land and resource practices; cultivating country; Dreaming; fire in Indigenous culture; Indigenous culture; Indigenous knowledges; land care
Crayfish, the, 13, 14
cultivating country
  Australian soils, 36, 67; and management, 39
  growing Indigenous plants, vegetables, 37, 38; apples,

other fruit, 55–7; cumbungi (ngurun) and water ribbon, 39, 40–1; grains and bread, 47, 58, 59–60, 61, **62–3**, 64–5; grasses, 45, 46, 47, 54, 57; herbage, 46–7; kurrajong, 57–8; selling to restaurants, 44; tubers, 46, 53, 54; warrigal greens and cunjim winyu, 42, 43–4; yam, 39

and history of agriculture, horticulture, 38, 53, 54, 55; farming native bees, 65–6

and justice for Indigenous people, 38, 45, 55–6, 59; opportunities, 65, 66; plants and intellectual property of Aboriginal people, 37, 56; wealth of Aboriginal skills, 37

new forest management, 36, 37, 47, 55; diversity, 36; sustainable, 74

use of fire, 40, 47, 52; cool burns, 47, 52

see also land care

Cunningham, Allan, 91–2

Curr, Edward, 39, 53, 75, 99, 124

Dampier, William, 161

Dangar, Henry, 137

Dawson, Robert, 134

Dooligah (ancestor/spirit), 23

Dreaming (*Tjukurpa*), 155

Country and creator spirits (ancestors), 82, 83, 95; and fire, 107, 110, 111, 126, 130; Rainbow Serpent, 119

and Law, 83; and ecology, 85

as religious philosophy, 83

and totems, 84–5, 97

Dumont d'Urville, JSC, 101

Ellis, Bob, 99, 100

Enlightenment, the, 43, 177, 179

Eyre, Edward, 92–3, 103

fire in Indigenous culture (1788 fire), 4–5, 22, 25, 73, 163, 166

alliance of fire and people, 106, 155; and ceremony, 107, 117, 121, 130, 149, 159; and community, 124, 126, 129, 149, 150

changed nature of fire and Country, 104–5, 106

cool fire, 29, 47, 52, 93, 95, 104, 123; for control, 109, 117–18, 130–1

distributing plants, 102; animals follow, 102

fire and ecology, 88–9, 93–4, 103, 134, 150, 163; and balance, 96, 100, 102, 159, 163, 167; creating clearings, 142; insects, 101; native grasses, 91–3, 112, 114, 117, 118, 121, 122; sustaining resources, diversity, 106, 127, 159, 163, 168; trees, plants, 89–91, 94, 122

fire and farming, 4, 8, 75; and control, 109–11, 116, 121, 131, 136, 141, 159; fires planned, guided, 106, 107, 121, 124,

126, 141, 143, 149; frequency, 111–12, 117, 118, (and timing), 113–17, 120, 122, 131; intensity of fire, 117–21; Law and rules, rituals, 83, 106, 107, 124, 126; management fires, 108–9, 126, 159; purpose, 87, 94–5, 97–8, 102–3, 105, 106, 108, 109, 114–15, 129; and random fire, 109, 110, 121, 136; templates, 109, 123–4, **125**, 126, (and dirty country), 126; whole of continent cared for, 109
fire terminology, 103–4
as a friend, 4, 86, 127, 162
and fuel reduction, 10–11, 52, 131, 143, 148; fuel rationed, 143
helping plants, animals, birds, 95–7, 98–9, 111, 122, 148, 163; fire as threat, 118; habitat, 148
hot fire, 118, 130, 136;
fighting, 132; preventing killer fires, 141
and 'no fire', 75–6, 87, 89, 91, 99, 102, 105, 123, 134, 159, 163, 167
protecting from fire, 95, 115, 127, 130–1; backburning, 130, 132
refreshing plant communities, 99–100
skill, knowledge, 97–8, 102, 117, 118, 122, 124, 128, 130, 149; loss of, 132; mosaics, 131, 152–3
suppressing, preventing fire, 100–1, 159
as a totem, 86; fire totem people, 106
see also Country

Forest Fire Behaviour Tables for Western Australia (Forests Department), 144–5
future farming
and harvesting roadkill, 70–1
protein exploitation, 67; kangaroos, emus, 68–9, 71; meat-eating and slaughter, 69; pelicans, 69; traditional herding method, 69, 70
and science, 73
seafood, 71; and harmful fishing methods, 71, 72; importance of seagrasses, 71; and overfishing, 71–2; and sustainability, 72–3, 74
see also cultivating country; loving Mother Earth

Gammage, Bill
The Biggest Estate on Earth, 10, 29, 142
Gerritsen, Rupert
Australia and the Origins of Agriculture, 33
Giles, Ernest, 101, 115
Gippsland
build-up of fuel, 153–4; fires in, 153, 154
see also Mallacoota
Grapes of Wrath, The (Steinbeck), 175
Grassie, James, 123–4
Grey, George, 39
Griffiths, Tom, 142
Gunn, RG, 88
Gurra (Aboriginal man), 82

Harrison, Chris, 57
Harvey, Musso, 116
Hellyer, Henry, 97
Holton, Mick, 145–6
Howitt, Alfred, 101
Howitt, William, 157
Hunter, John, 31, 32

Indigenous culture
  art, dance, song, 42, 85; and fire, 107, 129
  assumptions challenged, 8, 61
  ceremony, 11, 129; and fire, 107, 121; and harvests, 96; and interdependence of life and things, 11
  hunting, 114, 129; and fire, 121–2, 124
  innovation and adaptation, 8, 73
  Law, 76, 83, 86, 87, 162, 167
  lore, 23
  Songlines, 10; as elements of Country, ecology, 10, 85; and fire, 86, 155, 156
  spirituality and philosophy, 14, 31, 162
  story, 31; and fire, 107
  sustainable, 14, 73
  technology, building: artefacts, 70; the boomerang, 8, 56; built dwellings, 8; spears, net traps, 69
  see also Dreaming
Indigenous knowledges, 7–8, 65
  archive of, 8
  loss during frontier period, 41
  old people's knowledge, 58, 64, 126, 166; hunting and herding, 69; and Western sciences, 7, 61, 64
  and story, 31
  see also fire in Indigenous culture
Indigenous peoples, 3, 7
  as agriculturalists, 3, 32
  earliest occupation of Australia, 6, 31, 37, 190
  influences of Indigenous cultures on Australian society, history, 7

Jickling, Henry, 134
Jones, Rhys, 97
Joss, David, 124
Jurskis, Vic, 154

Kimber, Dick, 95–6, 115
Kirby, James, 39, 40

land care (present and future), 37
  farming and gardening, 3, 27, 28, 54; Aboriginal people in agriculture, 34, 38; fire-resistant plants, 28; growing crops, 25, 38, 182; grasses, 22, 27, 28, 32, 34, 173; tubers, 27; removing hard-hoofed animals, 28, 38, 173; and sustainability, 24; use of fire, 38, 103; vegetables, 22, 38
  forests, 22, 55; and fire, 23, 26–7, 52, 181, 182; and food grasses, 34, 182; management, 22, 24,

29–30, 35, 173, 181–2, (more open forests, parks), 182; native animals in, 30, 182–3; old people's ring trees, 24; plants, 28–9; recovery, 27–9; recycling timber, 182; a sustainable industry, 182
grazing game animals, 23
managing Country, 1–2, 7, 29, 32, 35, 114, 161; agriculture, 32, 40, 41, 167, (allowing for low rainfall), 181; controlling cats, foxes, 173; distributing palms, tubers, grasses, 32; domestication, 33; ecosystem and trees, 56; farming without fences, 3, 4, 25, 87, 161, 167; farming and gardening, 32–3; fostering native animals, 173; and 'hunter-gatherer', 3, 8, 32, 134, 167; manipulating water flows, 32; and sustainability, 1; tilling and harvesting, 3, 32
and sustainable power, 12
weeding country, 54–5
see also cultivating country; fire in Indigenous culture
Leichhardt, Ludwig, 96, 102–3, 137
loving Mother Earth, 14–15, 185
applying Christian or Islamic principles, ethics, 174, 175–6, 177, 180
avoiding waste, 170, 184; forest timber, 170
and compromising our future
and education, 183, 184; teaching a truer history, 171, 172

modifying market capitalism, 174, 180, 184–5; better regulation of business, 177
reconciliation: Uluru Statement from the Heart and treaty, 184
seeing the world differently, 177, 185
sustainability: agriculture, 172, 173, 181, 183; alternative methods, 180–1; and Australia's population challenge, 12; and chemicals, 180; fisheries, 183; forest management, 181; in lifestyle, 184; love of country, 183; producing traditional Aboriginal foods, 172
valuing resources, 169, 177; mining and the public good, 171
see also land care

Macarthur, John, 136
MacCabe, Francis, 45, 46, 52
Plan of the Survey of the Genoa River, **48–51**, 152, 154
Mallacoota (Vic)
and Aboriginal presence, 45, 46; agricultural zones, 47; early map of area, 45–6, **48–51**, 152; fire-management practices, 154–5
build-up of fuel levels, 153, 154; and control burns, 52, 153, 154; firestorm of 2019–20, 154, 181
parks, forest and undergrowth, 52, 154; and bird habitat, 52
preserved areas, 47
see also cultivating country; land care

Mannalargenna (Aboriginal man), 83
Marrngawi, Dinah, 126
Menge, Johannes, 101
Meza, Roberto, 172
Mitchell, Thomas, 39, 58, 76, 98, 111–12
  regrets absence of fire, 136–7
Mollison, Bill, 100
Morrison, Joe, 11
Morton, William, 92
Mullet, Russell, 45
Mulligan, John, 153, 154
Murray-Darling Basin
  fish kills, 181
  water rights, 73, 181

natural disasters in Australia
  and displacement of Indigenous people, 78, 139
  droughts, 30, 155
  fires (random), 25, 78, 109, 110, 113, 119, 139–40, 156, 157, 174; and commercial forestry, 22, 25; fire of 1851, 77; fires of 1939, 142, 153; fires of 1944, 144; fires of 1951, 157, 158; fires of 2019–20, 22, 23, 26–7, 28, 29, 47, 56, 145, 151, 154, 155, (impacts), 149, 156–7, 158, 165; in southern Australia, 159, 163; Western Australian fires, 144, 145
  lessons, 52
Newsome, Alan, 85
Nind, Scott, 121
Ninganga, Ida, 126

O'Malley, King, 189
O'Reilly, Bernard
  Green Mountains, 16

Pascoe, Bruce
  Dark Emu, 33, 59
Pelletier, Narcisse, 122
Péron, François, 101, 119–20
Phillip, Arthur, 42
Pring, Adele
  Women of the Centre, 179
Purula, Walter Smith, 115

religion
  and natural world as dominion of humans, 21, 176; consequences, 21
Robinson, GA, 46, 124
Rogers, JC, 140
Rolls, Eric, 137
royal commissions into fires, 142, 144, 166
Ruddy, Craig, 172

science and technology (non-Indigenous), 12–13
  agriculture and excess, 175; land clearing, 175
  capitalism, 12, 14, 18, 19, 174; and respect, 175
  Industrial Revolution, 15
  mining and disasters, 15, 174, 175
  misuses, 14; overfishing, 17, 18
  pollution, 15

science and war, 178–9
waste, 12, 14, 74
Scott, Lew, 139
Shewry, Ben, 44
Singh, Gurdip, 31
Singleton, Francis, 135
Stokes, John Lort, 110
Strehlow, Ted, 82
Stretton, Leonard, 142, 144
Sturt, Charles, 58, 88, 93
Sutton, Peter, 31, 33
Sydney Morning Herald, 161–2

Tairmunda (Williamy), 134–5
Tasmania
  and the Black Line, 83
  removal of people to Flinders Island, 138
Thomas, Ian, 99, 100
Thomas, Jamie, 42
Thomas, Mary, 120
Thomas, William, 84
Tjariya (Aboriginal woman), 146
Townsend, Thomas Scott, **125**
Turnbull, Malcolm, 184

Vader, John
  Red Gold, 16
Vancouver, George, 96
Victoria
  history of bushfires from 1851, 157–8
Victorian Forestry Commission, 154
  no-fire policy, 153; and fire of 1939, 153

von Hügel, Charles, 90

Walshe, Kerryn, 33
Watson, Don
  The Bush, 16
Watson, Judy, 60
Wills, William, 59

Yibarbuk, Dean, 126, 129
Young, Frank, 114
Yumburra. *See* land care; Mallacoota

Praise for the First Knowledges series …

'This beautiful, important series is a gift and a tool. Use it well.'
—Tara June Winch

'An in-depth understanding of Indigenous expertise and achievement across six fields of knowledge.'
—Quentin Bryce

'Australians are yearning for a different approach to land management. Let this series begin the discussion. Let us allow the discussion to develop and deepen.'
—Bruce Pascoe

'These books and this series are part of the process of informing that conversation through the rediscovery and telling of historic truths with contemporary application … In many ways, each individual book will be an act of intellectual reconciliation.'
—Lynette Russell

The best of both worlds

TITLES IN THE FIRST KNOWLEDGES SERIES

SONGLINES
Margo Neale & Lynne Kelly
(2020)

DESIGN
Alison Page & Paul Memmott
(2021)

COUNTRY
Bill Gammage & Bruce Pascoe
(2021)

ASTRONOMY
Karlie Noon & Krystal De Napoli
(2022)

PLANTS
Zena Cumpston, Michael-Shawn Fletcher & Lesley Head
(2022)

LAW
Marcia Langton & Aaron Corn
(2023)

Published in conjunction with the National Museum of Australia
and supported by the Australia Council for the Arts.